Punishment, danger and stigma

The morality of criminal justice

Punishment, danger and stigma

The morality of criminal justice

Nigel Walker

BARNES & NOBLE BOOKS
Totowa, New Jersey

First published in the USA 1980 by
Barnes and Noble Books
81 Adams Drive, Totowa, New Jersey, 07512

British Library Cataloguing in Publication Data

Walker, Nigel, *b. 1917*
   Punishment, danger and stigma.
   1. Punishment
   I. Title
   364.6'01   HV8675
   ISBN 0-389-20129-4

Printed in Great Britain.

Contents

Preface

This book may be seen as an attempt to undermine all three of the main justifications of punishment: retributive, reductive, denunciatory. Certainly it should convince readers that denouncers are really either quasi-retributivists or crypto-reducers. On the other hand, it argues that you cannot, at the end of the day, floor the retributivist. You may force him to concede that his justification rests on a very formal, rule-bound foundation. You can certainly face him with the implications of his view in matters such as mitigation, aggravation, stigma and offenders' rights; and then see if he likes them. But you cannot dismiss him.

Nor can you dismiss the reducer, who sees penalties (not 'punishments', a word with retributive implications) as instruments for reducing the volume of crime. You can face him with disappointing findings about the efficacy of his measures, although these findings are not quite as damaging as his opponents make out. You can make him unpopular by pointing to some of the implications of his view in matters such as stigma and offenders' rights, just as you can make the retributivist look old-fashioned by the same manoeuvre. But it is very difficult to argue that sentencers should never hope for practical results.

So the book is not meant to be entirely destructive: only to make the contestants face up to findings, implications and awkward questions. For what jurisprudes call 'the theory of punishment' tends to deal with a rather theoretical sort of punishment, which always achieves its intentions and never has any unwanted side-effects. On the other hand, the theorists can fairly accuse the more realistic penal reformers — whether they believe in just deserts, in improved treatment or merely in human rights — of ignoring the need for a tenable justification for penal measures, rather than slogans.

I realise that 'theory' is a word which makes Anglo-American judges push back their safety-catches, in contrast to the more reflective approach of their European colleagues. They may, however, be encouraged to find that this book takes seriously the 'eclectic' approach to sentencing which most of them have adopted: the view that some sentences are justifiable as retributive punishment, others in other ways. This is not necessarily mere opportunism. There is no obvious reason why every sentence must have the same justification. But if they want to stick to their eclecticism they must face its problems, which include all the problems of retributivism and reductivism, as well as a special one of its own.

It is not only practising lawyers, however, who distrust logical argument about punishment. Some sociologists, too, regard it as beside the point. (Others mistake it for sociology, having confused illustrations with descriptions.) For those who regard it as beside the point the important question seems to be 'With what ideology is this or that position associated?' The possibility that one viewpoint might be more reconcilable with what can be managed in practice, or have fewer internal contradictions, appears to be a minor consideration.

The point can be illustrated by my final chapter on offenders' rights (or 'prisoners' rights to those who prefer slogans). The rhetoric of rights has achieved so many improvements in the human condition that to point out some of its limitations is bound to seem either reactionary or Marxist. In fact scepticism about the status of 'natural' rights, or their inalienable quality, is not a symptom of any specific ideology. It is the converse that is true: belief in natural rights is more likely to be found amongst certain sorts of Christian. Nor, again, need scepticism be completely destructive. As I suggest at the end of the book, there is at least one constructive principle that does not beg so many questions.

The Cambridge Institute of Criminology   Nigel Walker

Acknowledgements and apologies

The various sections of this book have benefitted greatly from information, comments and references given to me by colleagues, friends, students and visitors to the Institute of Criminology. I hope that the following list includes them all:

Dr Andrew Ashworth (Oxford)
Dr Deryck Beyleveld (Sheffield)
Paul Nadin-Davis (Ottawa)
Professor Gil Geis (California)
Judge Sten Hekscher (Sweden)
Dr Barbara Huber (West Germany)
Birthe Jorgensen (Canada)
Professor Lopez-Rey (United Nations)
Dr Elizabeth Moberly (Cambridge)
Ronald Price, Q.C. (Canada)
Dr Marianne Schiøler (Denmark)
Jane Skelsey (New Zealand)
David Thomas (Cambridge)
Dr Warren Young (New Zealand)
Graham Zellick (London)

I am also grateful to the following publishers for raising no objection to the reproduction in this book — with much revision — of passages written by me which they originally published:

Edinburgh University Press (*Treatment and Justice: the Sandoz Lecture*, 1976).
Penguin Books (pages 41—59 of *Sentencing in a Rational Society*, 1969, 1972).

Pergamon Press (part of 'Dangerous People': the Kenneth Clarke Memorial Address, 1977, from the *International Journal of Law and Psychiatry,* I, 1, 37ff).

Sweet and Maxwell ('Punishing, reducing and denouncing crime' from *Reshaping the Criminal Law,* 1978, edited by Peter Glazebrook, and 'The Efficacy and Morality of Deterrents' from the March 1979 issue of the *Criminal Law Review*).

I have made some critical references to books such as *Doing Justice* and *Fair and Certain Punishment* (how can one be certain or fair?) because their titles are deliberately chosen for their appeal to moral principles, and they are therefore legitimate targets. Fortunately both books were the work of committees, so that even if I am shooting fish in a barrel I am doing it with a shotgun, and not aiming at individuals. As for the sentencers whose impulsive remarks in court I have occasionally quoted with something less than approval, I have deliberately not named them, even when tempted to stigmatise the stigmatisers in Chapter 7. The pronouncements of appellate courts are another matter: they are written in cold blood.

I see no need to apologise for occasionally differing from what I wrote ten years ago in *Sentencing in a Rational Society.* I would be more apologetic if I were simply repeating myself.

Finally, I owe a great many thanks to my secretary, Mrs Paige, for typing and good-temperedly retyping so many drafts, and to Miss Guy, the Administrative Secretary at the Institute of Criminology, for the care and accuracy with which, in her spare time, she prepared the final version for the press.

1 Criminalising

In any society which has advanced beyond the most primitive stage of development there is an institution for dealing with types of strongly disapproved conduct. In Western Europe it is usually called 'penal law'; in Britain 'the penal system'; in the U.S.A. and Canada 'the law enforcement system'. The things which must or can be done to individuals who engage in those types of conduct are prescribed by 'penal codes', although there is an increasing tendency for such systems to countenance alternatives: the chief of these are the handing over of certain categories of transgressor — such as juveniles or the mentally disordered — to other social institutions, and the 'diversion' of less well-defined categories to unofficial programmes for their rehabilitation.

The main subject of this book is neither the definitions of criminal codes nor the nature of the things which are done to people under these systems, but the justifications, whether explicit or implicit, for what is done. The first step, however, which requires a justification is the inclusion of a type of conduct in the criminal law: what is conveniently, if inelegantly, called 'criminalising' it. It may seem a little artificial to consider the justification for the inclusion of such actions as murder, rape, or robbery, which have for centuries been crimes in every jurisdiction worth the name. For one of the striking features of criminal codes is that in societies with widely differing histories and values the resemblances between their definitions of serious crimes are more extensive than the differences. To some extent this is attributable to the way in which successive empires have inherited, preserved and spread the principles of Roman law; but history cannot entirely account for it, and there seems to be something about human actions and reactions which promotes rather than undermines the similarity.

Yet even if the similarities are more impressive, it is the dissimilarities which raise interesting issues. What is more, the second half of this century has seen a new phenomenon. The scope of criminal codes had been (and still is) increasing: new offences were being added every year. In the nineteenth century one or two rather unorthodox thinkers — notably John Stuart Mill — had questioned the assumption that legislators were right in using the criminal law so indiscriminately. It was not until after the 1939—45 war, however, that this critical point of view was taken seriously by legislators. In England the issues which brought the controversy into real life were attempted suicide, abortion and male homosexuality: in the U.S.A. they were 'prohibition' and narcotics control.

Once people had been sensitised to the issue they began to debate other prohibitions: euthanasia, obscenity, birth control, artificial insemination, bigamy, sexual intercourse with minors. A bibliography of decriminalisation would give the impression that our civilisation was preoccupied by sex and death.

Is it possible to discuss the proper content of the criminal law in general terms? If the contents of criminal codes are examined with a sociological eye, no less than thirteen different objectives can be discerned:

    (1) the protection of human persons (and to some extent animals also) against intentional violence, cruelty or unwelcome sexual approaches;

    (2) the protection of people against some forms of unintended harm (for example, from traffic, poisons, infections, radiation);

    (3) the protection of easily persuadable classes of people (that is, the young or the weak-minded) against the abuse of their persons or property (for example, by sexual intercourse or hire-purchase);

    (4) the prevention of acts which, even if the participants

are adult and willing, are regarded as 'unnatural' (for example, incest, sodomy, bestiality, drug 'trips';

(5) the prevention of acts which, though not included under any of the previous headings, are performed so publicly as to shock other people (for example, nakedness, obscene language, or heterosexual copulation between consenting adults which takes place in public);

(6) the discouragement of behaviour which might provoke disorder (such as insulting words at a public meeting);

(7) the protection of property against theft, fraud or damage;

(8) the prevention of inconvenience (for example, the obstruction of roads by vehicles);

(9) the collection of revenue (for example, keeping a motor-car or television set without a licence);

(10) the defence of the state (for example, espionage or – in some countries – political criticism);

(11) the enforcement of compulsory benevolence (for example, the offence of failing to send one's child to school);

(12) the protection of social institutions, such as marriage or Christian worship (for example, by prohibiting bigamy or blasphemy);

(13) the enforcement of the processes regarded as essential to these other purposes (for example, offences connected with arrest, assisting offenders to escape conviction, and testimony at trials).

These objectives are so diverse that it may seem out of the question to formulate any general principles which will help to decide whether a given sort of behaviour should or should not be treated as a crime. For example, we are several centuries past the era in which the criminal law was thought of simply as the secular institution for the punishment of moral wrongdoing (if indeed this ever was wholly true) and we now recognise that many sorts of conduct which we condemn

morally are outside its scope, while other sorts within its
scope are from the moralists's point of view trivial, neutral
or even defensible.

Does this mean, however, that it is impossible to formulate any rules or principles to which we can appeal if we are
asked to decide whether a new crime should be created or an
old one abolished? Is the issue to be decided simply by the
strength of feeling that can be aroused amongst legislators
at an opportune moment? Certainly this is how many such
decisions have been taken in this century over the last hun-
dred years. In England the crime of 'gross indecency between
males' was created in 1885 by Henry Labouchère, a back-
bench member of Parliament who – for some reason which
has never been satisfactorily explained – successfully moved
this amendment to a bill which was designed to protect
immature girls from sexual exploitation. The crime of incest
was created in 1908 in response to pressure from the Church
of England, which had only recently begun to discover how
many slum-dwellers were unaware of the prohibitions of
Leviticus, Chapter 18. The Litter Act of 1957 was the result
of a private member's bill, supported by the Association for
the Preservation of Rural England. The Hypnotism Act 1952,
which prohibits stage hypnotists from using subjects under
the age of 21, was the result of a single unfortunate incident
in the Brighton Hippodrome.

It is easy by examples such as these to discredit our
present method of drawing and redrawing the boundaries of
criminal law. Is it possible to improve on it?

LIMITING PRINCIPLES

Now and again there have been attempts to formulate what
might be called 'limiting principles', which declare that the
criminal law should not be used for certain purposes, or in
certain circumstances.

The oldest seems to be

(A) Prohibitions should not be included in the criminal law for the sole purpose of ensuring that breaches of them are visited with retributive punishment.

It is probably not too far-fetched to ascribe this principle to Beccaria, whose *Of Crimes and Punishments* (1764) was the first treatise on penal theory to deal with the subject on utilitarian premises. His assertion that 'It is better to prevent crimes than to punish them. This is the ultimate end of all good legislation...' is the assumption with which the approaches of all later utilitarians, such as Bentham, Mill and Baroness Wootton, begin.

A few years later, Bentham's *An Introduction to the Principles of Morals and Legislation* (1789) stated three more limiting principles. The first was

(B) The criminal law should not be used to penalise behaviour which does no harm.

In his phraseology, punishment was groundless when, on the whole, there was no evil in the act. It is a principle to which everyone would give general assent, and would agree that it was the reason why we do not use the law to discourage bad manners or bad art. Nevertheless there would be many disagreements over other sorts of conduct. The idea of prohibiting bad art by law sounds ridiculous, but one of the things which town and country planning legislation tries to control is bad architecture, and a man who flouts it can suffer heavy penalities. How offensive must blasphemy be, and to how many people, before it is counted as harmful?

Another of Bentham's principles was

(C) The criminal law should not be used to achieve a purpose which can be achieved as effectively at less cost in suffering.

For instance, suggested Bentham, if the objection could be achieved 'by instruction...as well as by terror', terror should not be used. The trouble about this principle is that Bentham talks as if deterrence and instruction were interchangeable so far as everyone in a given class is concerned. He may simply have meant, of course, to exempt from punishment

very young offenders who needed only to be warned that
what they had done was a crime. But if he meant, as he
probably did, to exclude whole classes of harmful conduct
from the criminal law, he overlooked the possibility that
some of the people who indulge in such conduct might
respond to deterrence but not instruction. A better formu-
lation of the principle would be

> (CC) The criminal law should not be used where measures
> involving less suffering are as effective or almost as
> effective in reducing the frequency of the conduct
> in question.

Bentham's third principle was

> (D) The criminal law should not be used if the harm done
> by the penalty is greater than the harm done by the
> offence.

For in such cases punishment would be 'unprofitable' when
the felicific balance-sheet was added up. The difficulty about
this principle is that it requires us to weigh, let us say, the
unhappiness caused by bad architecture against the unhappiness caused by a large fine. Since the two sorts of unhappiness are inflicted on different people we cannot simply leave
it to individual choice, as we do when we ask someone
whether he would rather be fined or imprisoned. The difficulty of choosing between incommensurables is one of the
weaknesses of Benthamism which have been exploited by its
opponents.

A variant of this principle, however, seems to underlie a
modern argument that has been used against the wholesale
prohibition of abortion or homosexual acts. It has been
pointed out that such sweeping laws give rise to practices
which, on any point of view, are more undesirable than those
against which they are aimed. If legal abortions were not so
difficult to arrange, there would not be a black market in
illegal ones, with its high mortality. The outlawing of private
homosexual behaviour between consenting men provided
excellent opportunities for blackmail. The undiscriminating
prosecution of bigamists must have endangered many unions

between men and women which, though unhallowed, were stable and happy. The prosecution of narcotic addicts is said by sociologists such as Dr Schur (1963) to turn them into criminals. If Bentham had written today his comment would probably have been that

(DD) The criminal law should not include prohibitions whose by-products are more harmful than the conduct which they are intended to discourage.

Unfortunately this involves the same difficulty as principle D, although to a lesser degree. For principle DD is of help only when the prohibited conduct is so clearly less harmful than the by-products of the prohibition that there can be little disagreement on the subject. It is not surprising, therefore, to find that principle DD is invoked only when the conduct under discussion is of a kind which makes it possible to maintain either that the harm which it does is illusory or negligible, or that it harms only the person who indulges in it. It has been argued, for example, that marijuana-smoking is not in itself harmful to the body or mind, and that what does harm is the black market, created by the prohibition, which leads marijuana-smokers to associate with criminals, and especially with sellers of 'hard' drugs.

Others would argue that even if drug use is harmful — and there can be little doubt that some drugs are destructive — they harm only the user, who has freely chosen to use them (often, it is added, as an escape from some other kind of misery). Bentham himself recognised the existence of what he called 'self-regarding offences', which harmed only the offender, and which he thought it 'inexpedient' to punish. It was Mill, however, who in 1859 developed this into a full-blown principle in his essay *On Liberty*:

'The object of this Essay is to assert one very simple principle, as entitled to govern absolutely the dealings of society with the individual in the way of compulsion and control, whether the means used be physical force in the form of legal penalties or the moral coercion of public opinion. That principle is that the sole end for which mankind are warranted, individually or collectively, in interfering with the liberty of action of any of their number, is self-protection. That the only purpose for which power can be rightfully exercised over any member of a civilised community, against his will, is to prevent harm to others. His own good, either physical or moral, is not a sufficient warrant.'

Leaving aside for the moment the fact that Mill was talking about other forms of coercion as well as the law, a modern statement of his assertion might be this:

(E) The criminal law should not be used for the purpose of compelling people to act in their own best interests.

Mill himself recognised that there should be exceptions to this rule. 'Despotism', he thought, 'is a legitimate mode of government in dealing with barbarians provided that the end be their improvement'; and he took much the same view of the upbringing of children. So far as children were concerned, therefore, he would not have said that his principle ruled out compulsory benevolence such as enforced attendance at school.

What he himself had in mind were 'infringements of liberty' such as legal restrictions on the sale of poisons, on drunkenness unaccompanied by violence, on gambling and on Sunday amusements. He was not concerned with the question whether these were morally wrong or not; he was arguing that even if they were wrong nobody should attempt to use the law – or indeed the pressure of public opinion – to discourage others from such behaviour, since it did no harm to anyone except possibly the drug-addict, the drinker or the gambler himself. Other would-be reformers of the law have of course gone further, and argued that some of the acts which the law prohibits on the assumption that they are morally wrong are not wrong at all, or wrong only in special circumstances. Suicide, euthanasia, gambling, drinking, drug-taking, abortion and private homosexual behaviour have all been defended in this way. If their defenders had used Bentham's language they would have said that in such cases punishment is 'groundless'. For Mill, however, this was not the point. Whether such behaviour was wrong or not, the law should not be used against it.

Mill's principle has gained wide support in this country over the last century, probably because of its emotional appeal to a freedom-loving intelligentsia rather than the strength of the reasoning on which it was based. He himself thought that the strongest argument for it was that although an 'over-ruling majority' was likely to be right more often than not about conduct that affected the interests of other people, when it came to 'self-regarding conduct' it was quite as likely to be wrong as right: and he cited a number of obviously ridiculous discrepancies between the moral beliefs of different religions and cultures. He seems to imply that if a majority was in fact in the right it would be justified in interfering with self-regarding conduct. A stronger argument would have been that the object of such interference is usually to force people to behave morally, but that – as Professor Hart has pointed out (1965) – there is no virtue in morality if it is imposed from without.

Mill also had to meet the counter-argument that many of the types of behaviour which he wished to protect against interference were not, in the long run, self-regarding after all. As our subsequent experience has emphasised, the drinker, the drug-user, the gambler are likely to cause suffering to their dependants, relatives, and friends and to become eventually a burden which society has to carry. Mill's answer was rather forced and moralistic:

'I cannot consent to argue the point as if society had no means of bringing its weaker members up to its ordinary standard of rational conduct, except waiting till they do something irrational and then punishing them, legally or morally, for it. Society has had absolute power over them during all the early portion of their existence;

it has had the whole period of childhood and nonage in which to try whether it could make them capable of rational conduct in life.'

If (he is saying) society has failed to take its opportunity of ensuring that their upbringing protects them against the temptations of drink, drugs and gambling, it should not try to remedy its failure by punishing them when they are adults.

The argument is at once utopian, perfectionist and penologically out-of-date. Utopian because it assumes that society can control the upbringing of children and teenagers to this extent. Perfectionist because it asserts that if one has failed to achieve something desirable in the best way one should not be allowed to try the next best (an odd principle). Penologically out-of-date because it overlooks the possibility that the law might be a means – perhaps the only means – of compelling the alcoholic, the drug-addict or the gambler to undergo therapeutic treatment (Mill himself was of course writing in an era of deterrent penal measures, and could hardly be expected to envisage this).

THE PRAGMATIC APPROACH

The principles which Beccaria, Bentham and Mill formulated were moral prescriptions, which said that the penal system ought not to attempt this or that task. Other writers, however, were pursuing a more pragmatic line of thought and asking what the law could reasonably be expected to achieve. This is how Montesquieu approached the subject in Book XIX of *The Spirit of the Laws*. He recognised that prohibition by law can be carried further in some societies than in others, but thought that in any kind of society there were areas of conduct (which he called 'les moeurs et les manières') in which it was most unwise to use the law in the hope of effecting changes.

Even Mill's most violent opponent, the Victorian judge

James Fitzjames Stephen, accepted pragmatic limits of this
sort to the interference of the criminal law. In *Liberty,
Equality, Fraternity* (1973), which was a bitter attack on
Mill's essay, he admitted that 'you cannot punish anything
which public opinion, as expressed in the common practice
of society, does not strenuously and unequivocally condemn.
To try to do so is a sure way to produce gross hypocrisy
and furious reaction'.

In the less emotional language of the twentieth century
this principle might read

(F) The criminal law should not include prohibitions
which do not have strong public support.

The principle has its own weaknesses — such as the difficulty
of measuring public opinion in a morally pluralistic society.
Like Mill's principle its justification is not self-evident, and
it raises the question 'Why not?'. Stephen's own reason seems
to have been 'because of the gross hypocrisy and furious
reaction which would result if one failed to observe this
principle'.

Whether Stephen could have supported his argument with
convincing examples is doubtful: certainly subsequent experience suggests that he overstated it. Our attempts to
improve people's driving of motor-cars by means of the
criminal law have certainly been made without the 'strenuous
and unequivocal condemnation' of public opinion. Each
successive attempt to strengthen penalties or improve means
of enforcing the law has met with organised opposition from
the motorists' associations. Admittedly some of their arguments might fairly have been regarded by Stephen as 'gross
hypocrisy': but this can scarcely amount to the 'furious
reaction' that he predicted.

The importance of Stephen's principle, however, lies in
the recognition that there are practical limits to the scope
of the criminal law. Bentham and Mill wrote as if there were
no difficulty in detecting and punishing any sort of offence,
even self-regarding ones; and their principles were moral
prescriptions. Punishment ought not to be inflicted if it is

groundless, needless, unprofitable or inefficacious, said Bentham; self-regarding offences ought not to be discouraged by law or any other form of coercion, thought Mill. Stephen, who was a lawyer and a judge, lifted the problem out of the armchair of moral philosophy and into the fresh air of practical politics. The fact that he was arguing in favour of punishing many offences which Mill would have exempted from the criminal law makes him, by modern standards, reactionary; but it does not mean that all he said should be disregarded.

On the contrary it is worth asking in the light of modern experience what are the practical, as distinct from the moral, considerations that suggest limits to the scope of criminal law?

An obvious practical consideration is the economics of enforcement. The chief agencies of enforcement are police forces, whose size is restricted by the amount of public money which the society in question is willing to spend on them. Even if this were not a limiting factor, it would be found that the number of suitable men and women willing to be recruited to the police was not large enough to make an enormous expansion possible. Allocating policemen's time to the best advantage will always be a major problem, but the extent to which it regulates the rigour of law enforcement is not fully appreciated. In many cities a report of a theft involving property of less than a certain amount is not even passed to the detective branch for fear of wasting their time.

Another important consideration is the law-enforcement agencies' need for the assistance of the private citizen. Apart from a selection of driving and parking offences, of revenue offences and breaches of health or safety regulations which can be detected and brought home to the offenders entirely by the observation and evidence of police, inspectors and other officials, very few offences would come to official knowledge if they were not reported by private citizens, and very few of these would be traced to their perpetrators if it were not for the information which the police are able to obtain from the same source.

There are some offences, indeed, which could seldom be prosecuted without the evidence of one of the participators. One of the reasons why women who have resorted to criminal abortionists are so seldom prosecuted in England is that their evidence is usually needed to secure the conviction of the abortionists. Again, most police forces are so determined to convict blackmailers that they will refrain from prosecuting the victims who give evidence against them.

One of the dangers inherent in the extension of the criminal law to a multitude of peccadilloes is that by making a larger percentage of the population into targets for law-enforcement agencies it may forfeit the co-operation of this percentage in the enforcement of the more important prohibitions. An obvious example of this possibility is traffic offences, which now account for the great majority of all convictions. It is impossible to assess the amount of co-operation which the law enforcement agencies forfeit by such prosecutions, but it must be considerable. The same is true of prosecutions for possession of marihuana.

Even when prosecutors could secure convictions without too much trouble they often refrain from doing so in cases where they believe that strict enforcement would alienate the public. In England, youths who can be proved to have had sexual intercourse with girls not far below the statutory age of consent (at present sixteen) are often not prosecuted, largely because the police feel that public opinion would not support them. Another rather unpopular indictment is bigamy, which in England is not prosecuted nowadays unless there is evidence that the guilty party went through the form of marriage in order to deceive the other party into having sexual intercourse or into parting with property. In countries where private homosexual behaviour between consenting adult men is still criminal, prosecutions for this are often restricted to cases in which there is evidence or suspicion of proselytising, commercial exploitation, blackmail or 'orgies'.

Another assumption which seems to underlie some arguments against certain prohibitions is that

(G) A prohibition should not be included in the criminal law if it is unenforceable.

The word 'unenforceable', however, is used very loosely in such arguments. Does it mean 'such that *some* breaches of it would not be detected'? Hardly, for in this sense every prohibition is unenforceable. Does it mean 'such that *all* breaches of it would be undetected'? Again, hardly; for it is no easier to think of any prohibition that would be unenforceable by this criterion. (Perhaps the nearest thing to a genuinely unenforceable prohibition in the history of English law was the form of treason which consisted of 'imagining' the death of the king, the queen or the heir apparent, before it became established by case-law that an overtly treasonable act must be proved.' What the principle must mean is that

(GG) A prohibition should not be included in the criminal code if only a small percentage of breaches of it could be proved against the perpetrators.

In this form the principle at once raises the question 'How small must the percentage be?', which is impossible to answer precisely, and not at all easy to answer even roughly until some reply has been given to the more fundamental question 'Why is relative unenforceability an argument against the inclusion of the prohibition?' The stock answer to this is that it 'brings the law into disrepute'.

Like so many stock answers this needs a very close examination. It can hardly mean that a complete absence of attempts to enforce a particular law discredits the whole criminal code, or law-enforcement agencies in general; for the history of every criminal code has plenty of instances in which prohibitions have been allowed to fall into desuetude, without any evidence that this weakened respect for the operative parts of the code. Does it mean that the agencies of law enforcement make themselves ridiculous by unsuccessful attempts to secure convictions? If so, this could be remedied very easily by taking action only when the prospects of succeeding are very good, as the police do with speeding offences.

A more plausible form of the argument might be that if those who are prosecuted for a given offence are regarded by their fellow-citizens as a small and unlucky selection from those who actually committed it, the public may come to feel that their prosecution is 'unfair'. That such a feeling might well be irrational — especially if the offenders knew that they were risking prosecution — would not prevent it from being widespread. Certainly offenders who are unlucky enough to be prosecuted for a commonly undetected offence — such as exceeding speed limits — seem to feel it.

At most, however, this would be an argument for extreme caution in actually prosecuting detected breaches of the prohibition, and not an argument against including the prohibition in the criminal code. For quite a strong argument can be put forward for retaining, or indeed inserting, even unenforceable prohibitions.

The argument is that the law influences conduct, not merely because people are deterred by the possible consequences of infringing it, but also because it is taken as a declaration of what the society in question condemns. This theory — which I have elsewhere called 'the declaratory theory' — resembles the denunciatory justification of penalties (see Chapter 2), but is distinguishable because it asserts that even if no one were ever penalised for a breach of a prohibition (indeed even if no one knew what the penalty was) it would still help to maintain standards of conduct.

Certainly the clearest examples of the use of this argument have been connected with prohibitions whose enforceability was doubtful at the very least. It was put forward to the Wolfenden Committee on Homosexual Offences and Prostitution by witnesses who were against the relaxation of the law on homosexual acts between men; and the sole member of the Committee who dissented from this relaxation expressed the objection by saying

'Many citizens ... regard the prohibitions expressly
imposed by law as the utmost limit set to their activities ... and the removal of the present prohibition
from the criminal code will be regarded as condoning
or licensing licentiousness...'[1]

At least one Home Secretary has used the argument to
defend legislation which was avowedly designed to influence
opinion rather than penalise conduct. During the second
reading of the Race Relations Bill of 1968 Mr Callaghan said

'I attach great importance to the declaratory nature of
the first part of the Bill. I believe that ... the very process
of giving the law brings an instinctive response from the
great majority of our citizens.' [Hansard, Commons,
23 April 1968.]

Whatever one's views on these particular laws may be, the
argument is not implausible. We know that in other areas of
opinion, such as politics, people are apt to alter their judgements to correspond with what they believe to be the view of
the majority. Experiments in which I have collaborated with
Mr Argyle and Professor Berkowitz[2] confirm that university
students' views on the morality of certain actions can be
strongly influenced by telling them the results of fictitious
opinion-surveys of their peers. Might not the criminal law
function as a powerful means of inducing people to believe
that a given type of conduct is strongly condemned by their
peers?

The same experiments, however, showed that in the case
of most students it was not possible to influence their moral
judgements by inducing them to believe that a given action
was or was not prohibited by the criminal law. Two reservations must be made at this point. One is that in both

---

[1] See Mr Adair's Minority Report appended to the main report.
[2] Walker and Argyle (1964); Berkowitz and Walker, (1967).

experiments there was a minority of students whose moral judgements probably were influenced in this way. In the first experiment these were identified as students who believed that if a law was passed, for example against heavy smoking, it became morally wrong to disobey that law. In the experiment designed by Berkowitz the minority was identified as students who were 'deeply involved in their society, traditional and conventional and socially responsible'. (In all probability the two experiments on different samples pointed to much the same sort of minority: the student who thought that legislation could *ipso facto* render an act morally wrong was probably a student who was also traditional, conventional and socially responsible.) An equally important reservation is that these experiments measured only short-term effects on a rather special sub-group of the population. They do not prove − and it is difficult to see what sort of experiment could prove − that alterations of the law do not have long-term effects on moral attitudes..

A POSITIVE JUSTIFICATION?

The thorough-going pragmatist, however, is one who abandons the defensive approach. Instead of merely setting up warning notices in the form of limiting principles which try − not very practically − to indicate to legislators where they should stop, he asks why the onus of proof should not lie on those who want to extend the scope of the criminal law. They should, on this view, be required to show why it is desirable. Shifting the burden of proof in this way has obvious difficulties. The very diversity of functions to which I have already drawn attention makes any attempt to approach the problem in this way sound naive. Nevertheless, if an institution is as costly − whether in terms of economic resources or of human happiness − as the penal system undoubtedly is, it seems more realistic to ask for positive justifications whenever it is to be used against a given sort of conduct.

If possible, these justifications should not appeal to moral sentiments of the sort that condemn certain kinds of behaviour. They should not assert that the criminal code should prohibit this or that because it is wicked. To assert this is to invite argument as to what is or is not wicked, and in any society — let alone one which contains a wide diversity of moral views as Britain — areas of disagreement will quickly be found.

Something like a non-moralistic justification was offered by Sir Patrick (now Lord) Devlin, in his well-known lecture on *The Enforcement of Morals* (1959), where he said

'The State must justify in some other way [than by reference to the moral law] the punishments which it imposes on wrongdoers and a function for the criminal law independent of morals must be found. This is not difficult to do. The smooth functioning of society and the preservation of order require that a number of activities should be regulated...'.

It was unfortunate that the main purpose of his lecture was to examine the Wolfenden Committee's recommendation that homosexual acts in private between consenting adults should not be criminal. For it led him to argue, in effect, that private homosexual acts between men might well arouse such 'general abhorrence' that they did in fact threaten our society with disintegration. This was so obviously unrelated to the social and political facts that — together with other weaknesses in his argument — it laid him open to telling attacks from Hart and other spiritual descendants of Mill.

Nevertheless, the misapplication of a principle does not necessarily invalidate it; and, however injudiciously, Devlin was in fact stating one of the main axioms of a philosophy which seems to underlie a good deal of modern penal legislation.

The need to ensure 'the smooth functioning of society' must, after all, be the main justification for the parts of the criminal code which are concerned with the protection of health, the collection of revenue and the defence of the realm — objectives 2, 9 and 10 on pages 2–3. Most, though probably not all, of the other prohibitions can be regarded as necessary for 'the preservation of order', to the extent at least that, if they were not enforced on some occasions, there would be disorder. Not all theft or damage would provoke public disturbances; some victims, for example, would be afraid to retaliate. But some would not, and their methods of protecting themselves or avenging their losses would lead to breaches of the peace. The same is true of intentional violence against the person or unwelcome sexual advances. The prohibition of these can be justified because they are classes of actions of which by no means all, but a substantial number, would provoke disorder.

Nevertheless there are some prohibitions which it is not very plausible to justify in this way. The obvious examples are in my group 4, which consists largely of sexual behaviour that has come to be regarded as 'unnatural', and is prohibited by many criminal codes even if it takes place in private, and between participants who are adult, sane and under no coercion or inducement other than their own desires. (It is interesting to note how difficult it is to think of any form of non-sexual behaviour that is regarded as so 'unnatural' as to call for the intervention of the criminal law. Coprophagy, for instance, strikes an enormous majority of people as unnatural, but is not prohibited in any criminal code of which I know.) So long as incest[3] or homosexual acts are genuinely private, and do not involve advertisement, coercion, deceit or

[3] Virtually all the prosecuted cases of incest involve fathers who have had intercourse with daughters who are under the age of consent, and could thus be prosecuted as unlawful sexual intercourse. It is incest between consenting adults which is hardly ever prosecuted and which could without loss be excluded from the criminal code, as lawyers such as Sir Rupert Cross (1963) have suggested. There are even countries — France and Belgium being examples — where incest of any kind is not a crime, but abuse of authority for sexual purposes is.

the persuasion of the young or mentally disordered, they are most unlikely to provoke disorder.

The difficulty of arguing, however, that such prohibitions are in the interests of public order or the smooth functioning of society is not an argument for seeking some other kind of justification. For it is just this sort of prohibition about which modern legislatures are uneasy. In the minority of civilised societies in which the criminal code still prohibits homosexual behaviour between consenting adult males, the prohibition seems to be enforced with less and less enthusiasm or efficiency, and its justification is questioned with increasing frequency.

At first sight there is another category of penal legislation which is not easy to justify on Devlin's principle: what I have called 'compulsory benevolence'. It is implausible to argue that the evasion of universal education or national schemes of social insurance is likely to lead to breaches of the peace. It is not so unrealistic, however, to suggest that children who are allowed to grow up illiterate or more than usually ignorant in a technological society, or people who make no provision for sickness or old age, become economic burdens on their society, and perhaps nuisances of other kinds. This being so, compulsory benevolence can fairly be said to be in the interests of the 'smooth functioning' of society.

Without discussing all the frontiers of the criminal code in detail, I have tried to show that it is not out of the question to formulate both limiting principles and positive justifications which are considerably less dependent on moralistic assumptions and values than, for example, Mill's principles. It is true that they are no more precise. There is just as much room for argument as to what is necessary for the smooth functioning of society or the preservation of order as there is over the question of what is or is not a purely self-regarding offence. But whereas arguments over self-regarding offences are apt to end in deadlock between two or more moral viewpoints, disputes as to what is or is not detrimental to smooth functioning or order do allow for some sort of appeal to observable fact and experience.

It must also be admitted that instead of attempting, like Mill, to draw an eternal boundary between what may and what may not properly be regulated by official sanctions, Devlin offers only a shifting frontier. What may provoke disorder in one generation or one society may not do so in a more tolerant one. In a society which is thrown into a panic by rumours of witchcraft it may be desirable – in a peace-keeping sense – to prohibit witchcraft, as colonial administrators found in Africa. This does not mean, of course, that the prohibitions should be enforced by mediaeval penalties. What it does mean is that those who see no harm in witchcraft must make some progress in communicating their enlightened viewpoint to the society in question before demanding the abolition of the law that prohibits it.

Can it be argued, however, that the demand for a positive justification based on the smooth functioning of society and the preservation of order is completely value-free? In the first place, it assumes that the society in question is one that should be allowed to function in an orderly way. Some people regard some societies as so iniquitous or inequitable as to make this a misguided objective. This can be conceded, however, without surrendering the whole approach. It is quite consistent to hold that for those who believe in a given sort of society a sensible objective of the criminal law is to promote its orderly functioning, but that for those who object to that kind of society disobedience is a rational technique for changing it. This can be read as a mere sociological observation; but it is also a logical point. If we regard the criminal law as simply an instrument designed for this limited purpose, both the values of the society which it serves and the values of the enemies of that type of society are outside the scope of this particular argument. This does not imply that those who breach the criminal law in attempts to change or overthrow a society have a claim to be exempt from its penalties. It is possible to argue that the penalties are excessive, or even that political motives should be a mitigating circumstance when people kill or rob, without holding that deliberate homicide or robbery should not be penalised.[4]

One interesting feature distinguishes the pragmatists's approach which I have just been discussing from the moralist's approach. Suppose that both are agreed in disapproving very strongly of some type of conduct. For the pragmatist the question is simply whether on balance anything useful would be achieved by invoking the criminal law against it. The moralist, however, seems to agonise in a special way over this step. He may be willing to see all sorts of other steps taken to reduce the frequency of the conduct – education, propaganda, restriction of opportunities – and yet may consider it morally wrong to use the criminal law in the campaign.

It is hard to see, however, what it is that in the moralist's eyes distinguishes the criminal law. It may of course be simply that he regards its penalties as excessively severe; but that is not an essential feature of the criminal law. Would he still object if a fine were the maximum penalty for whatever conduct is in question? If so, perhaps it is the stigma of conviction that worries him? But stigma is not inseparable from conviction, as we shall see in Chapter 7. It might perhaps be that the criminal law seeks to *compel* whereas other techniques of social control work by persuasion or indoctrination. This seems an undeniable distinction, which appeals to one's instinctive dislike of being ordered to do do something, even if it is in one's interests.

[4] The problem becomes more acute when an activity is prohibited only because of its political meaning: when a book is banned or a demonstration forbidden because of the message which it is intended to convey. The 'right to free speech' has been powerfully asserted in Britain and the U.S.A., although when claimed by groups such as racists or paedophiles it has worried even some liberals.

It raises two questions, however. Are all other techniques of social control less objectionable morally than the compulsion of the criminal law? Is one-sided indoctrination – for example against birth-control – any better? The second question is whether a strong and sincere belief in the harmfulness – or sinfulness – of the conduct does or does not create a duty to do what one can to prevent it, short of doing even greater harm. Whether or not one takes sides on this issue, it is clear that the moralist has a choice between three positions, two simple and one complex:

a. he may hold sincere and well-defined views about the wrongness of conduct and yet think it wrong to try to influence the behaviour of others by *any* means (a fairly rare position);
b. he may on the other hand think it justifiable, even obligatory, to seek to influence the behaviour of others by *any* means;
c. he may take position (b) but hold that *some* means are ruled out.

Note that (c) involves ruling out certain *means*, not certain types of conduct. The difficulties – for the moralist – of drawing distinctions between types of conduct which he may or must seek to eliminate and those which he should not have already been shown to be insuperable, if not in theory at least in practice. It is the techniques about which he has to worry.

Since the aim of this book is not to indoctrinate but to clarify issues, that is as far as this chapter can go. Those which follow deal with the moral aspects of the use of the criminal law as a technique of control, beginning with the rival justifications for the central feature of the criminal law: the penalising of those who infringe it.

2 Punishing, denouncing or reducing

'Certain things are simply wrong and ought to be punished. And this we do believe' (*Doing Justice*, Report for the Committee for the Study of Incarceration)

'Organising the future ... is not the major function of the criminal law. Even if we cannot control the future, this does not mean we must ignore the present and the past. We still need to do something about wrongful acts: to register our social disapproval, to publicly denounce them and to reaffirm the values violated by them' (*Our Criminal Law*, Law Reform Commission of Canada).

These two quotations, both from recent publications, illustrate the revival of interest in the retributive and the denunciatory justifications for punishment. This revival is a reaction against the utilitarian approach, which is becoming unpopular partly because of the excessive prison terms imposed in the United States in the name of rehabilitation or public protection, and partly because of discouraging evidence about the efficacy of sentences designed to reform or deter. Like other revivalists, however, latter-day preachers of these doctrines are slightly confused about what they are selling. The authors of *Doing Justice* seem unaware of most of the difficulties of retributivism. The Canadian Law Reform Commission's light-hearted appeal to denunciation, and their assumption that it is a non-utilitarian aim, is more excusable, since critical and thorough discussions of the concept are not easy to find.[1] Both publications, however, seem to demonstrate the need for an up-to-date review of the three rival justifications for inflicting penalities, and the difficulties which they raise even from a commonsense point of view. With apologies for covering some familiar ground, I must begin with a brief statement of each.

THE RETRIBUTIVE

This holds that the justification for inflicting a penalty is that the offender *deserves* it because of his offence. The pure retributivist also believes that the severity of the penalty should match the offender's culpability. Culpability varies according to the gravity of the harm done, intended or consciously risked, the offender's motives and any circumstances relevant enough to mitigate or aggravate it (see Chapter 6).

There are, however, modifications of this view. The 'limiting' retributivist does not insist that the severity of the penalty should match the offender's culpability; only that it should not exceed what would match it. In other words, the penalty could be the minimum necessary to achieve other aims (*e.g.,* deterrence) so long as it was not

---

[1] Professor H. L. A. Hart devotes a few not very sympathetic pages to it in *Punishment and Responsibility*, pp. 170–173. I gave it equally short shrift in *Sentencing in a Rational Society*. Professor J. Feinberg dealt with it sympathetically but incompletely in *Doing and Deserving*. Examples of earlier versions are to be found in Bernard Bosanquet's *Some Suggestions in Ethics,* and in Emile Durkheim's *Division of Labour in Society*. Better known to English lawyers is James Fitzjames Stephen's denunciatory argument about capital punishment in his *History of the Criminal Law of England,* which may have inspired Lord Denning to argue similarly to the Royal Commission on Capital Punishment in 1954. The Law Society used it (under the name 'D factor') in their evidence to the Royal Commission on the Penal System. The Court of Appeal have used it occasionally: for example in *Llewellyn-Jones* (1967) 51 C.A.R. 204; and see my quotation from *Sargeant* (1974) 60 C.A.R. 74, at n. 3, below.

excessively severe by retributive standards.

The other important version of the retributive point of view can be called 'distributive'. It insists merely that a penalty should not be inflicted on a person who has not culpably broken a rule. It does not insist that the severity of the penalty should either match or be limited by culpability. The principle 'no penalty without culpability' is observed, in theory at least, by all civilised penal codes, although many of them allow exceptions (as in the case of offences of 'strict liability').

Most penal codes are also constructed on lines consistent with limiting retributivism, providing *maximum* sentences which set the upper limit to severity without obliging the court to impose the maximum. (Many such systems, however, have obligatory penalties for a few offences, such as death or 'life' for murder, which are more consistent with the pure form of the retributive theory.) A few systems, such as the Scots', set no upper limit to the length of a prison sentence or the amount of a fine when imposed by the highest court, but even they honour the principle of 'no penalty without culpability'.

Limiting and distributive retributivists are able to compromise with holders of non-retributive points of view. Indeed, their views *imply* some other, non-retributive justification for penalities, since all they offer is principles for restricting punishment, not reasons for imposing it. Only the pure retributivist, who argues that penalties should be imposed because they are deserved, is offering a justification of them. I shall call such people 'punishers'.

THE UTILITARIAN (REDUCTIVE)

This holds that the justification for penalising offences is that this reduces their frequency. It is therefore more precise to call this the 'reductive' point of view, since utilitarians are really concerned with maximising the sum of human happiness, and could conceivably argue that penalties severe enough to make a real impact on the frequency of, say, motoring offences would generate more unhappiness than they would prevent. 'Reducers' believe that penalties reduce the frequency of offences in one or more of the following ways:

(i) deterring the offender (*i.e.*, inducing him to refrain from further law-breaking − or at least law-breaking of the same sort − by means of the memory of the penalty);

(ii) deterring potential imitators (*i.e.*, discouraging them from following the offender's example through fear of the penalty which he incurred);

(iii) reforming the offender (*i.e.*, improving his character so that he is less often inclined to commit offences even when he can do so without fear of the penalty);

(iv) educating the public to take a more serious view of such offences (thus indirectly reducing their frequency);

(v) protecting the public (or specific potential victims such as wives) by incapacitating offenders (*e.g.*, by long prison sentences).

Reducers can compromise with limiting retributivists by accepting maximum penalties, although these will occasionally interfere to some extent with their aims: for example by setting a limit to the length of protective custody. They can also compromise with the retributive principle of 'no penalty without culpability.' They are probably making a sacrifice by doing so, since it is generally believed that the efficacy of general deterrents would be maximised by ensuring that *someone* is penalised for every known crime, even if those who penalised were secretly aware that they were sometimes penalising the innocent (see p. 34). But by conceding that the innocent should not be knowingly penalised the reducer is not surrendering his position.

THE EXPRESSIVE (DENUNCIATORY)

This holds that the justification for penalising an offender is that doing so expresses an important statement about the offence. A penalty declares, in effect, that in the society in question the offence is not tolerated.[2] On the expressive view this is not sufficiently declared by laws which merely prohibit certain conduct: penalties must be provided and people must be sentenced.

It is important to be clear whether a 'denouncer' (as I shall call someone who holds this view) is really a 'reducer', or something else. If he believes that the point of declaring society's non-toleration of this or that sort of law-breaking is to strengthen people's disapproval of it, and so reduce its frequency, he is simply a reducer who belives in a particular technique: see *B*.iv.

If, on the other hand, the denouncer denies that he is a mere reducer, he must tell us what it is that makes the expression of non-toleration a good thing. Sociologically-minded denouncers usually give Durkheim's answer to this question: that denunciation promotes social cohesion. If this is offered as a justification (and not as a mere description) it is implied that social cohesion is a good thing, and the answer is again a utilitarian one, although rather vaguer and harder to test than the reductive version.

It is possible, however, to be a less utilitarian denouncer,

---

[2] Feinberg has pointed out other expressive functions which penalties *sometimes* perform. One is the absolution of other people who may have been under suspicion of the offence in question. The other is the declaration to another state that the punishing state disowns what the offender did, as when the pilot of a military aircraft makes an unauthorised attack on the aircraft of another state, and it becomes important to make it clear that the attack is not approved by his government. But these are not common situations. A more general version of the expressive justification, which he calls 'anti-impunity', is offered by Hyman Gross (1979) pp. 400ff. Earlier, however, on p. 5, he hints that he may really be an eclectic.

who justifies penalties by talking not of any future benefit but simply of the immediate satisfaction which they give to people who know and disapprove of the offence, in much the same way as funerals and other ceremonials give satisfaction to most if not all participants. This is probably the version of the expressive justification which comes nearest to being both non-utilitarian and non-retributive: I call it 'ceremonial denunciation'.

It should be easy to distinguish any version of the denunciatory justification from retributivism, although it is possible to confuse the two:

> ... I will start with retribution. The Old Testament concept of an eye for an eye and tooth for tooth no longer plays any part in our criminal law. There is, however, another aspect of retribution ...: it is that society, through the courts, must show its abhorrence of particular types of crime .... The courts do not have to reflect public opinion. On the other hand the courts must not disregard it. Perhaps the main duty of the court is to *lead* public opinion ....[3]

But that is by the way. In either form the expressive view is clearly distinguishable from the retributive. For if denunciation is to be achieved the penalty must be publicly announced, whereas retribution can be achieved by secret punishment.

Paradoxically, however, denouncers could not exist without retributivists. For the penalty could not have any of the effects in which denouncers believe (whether the giving of immediate satisfaction or the promotion of disapproval or social cohesion) unless the people upon whom it is meant to have this effect regarded it as just in the retributive sense. This paradox, however, does not imply

---

[3] The English Court of Appeal (Criminal Division) in *R. v. Sargeant* (1974) 60 Cr. App. R., 74.

that the expressive view is really retributivism after all; for the latter demands that the penalty be genuinely appropriate to the offender's culpability, or actually inflicted on a culpable offender, whereas all the denouncer can demand is that those at whom he aims his effect should *believe* it to be retributively appropriate. Moreover, he cannot logically demand that the penalty should actually be inflicted: merely that it should (i) he publicly ordered and (ii) be thought to have been inflicted.[4]

A few denouncers, however, have a more limited aim than influencing public opinion or giving satisfaction to those who are outraged by an individual offence. They see the penalty as a symbolic way of telling the offender something. That something may be either society's disapproval or the inherent wickedness of his act.[5] This view does not require that the penalty be publicised; but it seems to require that the offender himself believe that it is going to be inflicted, in order to make him take its symbolism seriously.

DECIDING BETWEEN THE THEORIES

It is usually assumed in academic discussions that one should adopt the same justification for all penalties for all offences. In practice, however, sentencers often appeal to different justifications in different circumstances, or for different penalties. Thus a judge might argue that certain offences (*e.g., mala in se*) should be punished for retributive (or expressive) reasons, while others (*e.g., mala prohibita*) should be penalised only for utilitarian reasons. There is nothing inherently illogical in this argument, so long as one can offer an explicit and plausible distinction between the situations in

---

[4] Perhaps he need not even insist on (ii): see my quotation from Thesiger, J., later in this chapter.

[5] This seems to be the main justification put forward by Dr. Elizabeth Moberly, the theologian.

which each justification is appropriate, and so long as one is not using the argument to allow one to justify what one really wants to do for other reasons (*e.g.,* personal dislike of, or sympathy for, the offender).

A problem arises, however, when two justifications clearly point to different ways of dealing with the same offender for the same offence. He may appear to deserve punishment, yet the sentencer may also have good reason to believe that imprisonment will increase the probability of his reoffending, and that a probation order would be better from the reductive point of view.[6] If the sentencer believes in both the retributive and the reductive justifications, how is he to make his choice? He can proceed in two ways. He may appeal to a rule which tells him to give priority to one of the justifications. An imaginary example would be: 'If some penalty seems likely to have a reductive effect, choose it; if not, sentence retributively.' He will not find such a rule in the textbooks, the statutes or case-law, so it is up to him whether to adopt it or not, and to defend his order of priority. But it would at least enable him to make choices with consistency.

Or he may say, 'When the offender seems very culpable I make a retributive choice; otherwise I act with an eye to reducing future offences,' implying that until a certain degree of culpability is reached he reasons reductively, but when it is reached he switches to the retributive justification. This is less rational than following an order of priority: it is not a rule but a reaction.

Some people talk of 'the' justification for penalties. This would make sense if there were considerable agreement on the subject. Since this is obviously not so, what does it mean? Possibly the justification which legislators or rule-makers had in mind when introducing a penalty. Yet even when it is possible to be sure of what they had in mind, this sometimes differs from what sentencers have in mind when imposing the

---

[6] Let us suppose, too, that the case is unlikely to be reported by the press, so that general deterrence is not a consideration.

penalty, and from what is in the minds of those who have to carry it out. The offender, too, may interpret the penalty in his own way. If a legislator's justification is reductive, but the sentencer's is expressive, and the penal agent's is retributive, whose is 'the' justification? Probably what is meant is 'the only tenable one'.

Is it possible, then, to show that two out of the three are untenable? It is certainly possible to show in special or particular cases that no sensible person could justify a penalty on this or that ground. It would, for instance, usually be difficult to call a probation order 'retributive' or 'expressive'. [7]

DISCREDITING JUSTIFICATIONS

What most[8] theorists of punishment, however, seem to be trying to do is to show why legislators (or some other kind of rule-maker) and sentencers should confine themselves to one or other of the justifications. In order to do so it is necessary to discredit the other possible justifications very thoroughly. Can this be done?

The denouncer can be attacked, as we have seen, on the ground that what he is justifying is not the actual penalising of offenders but the ceremonial pronouncement of a penalty. For his purpose it is sufficient if the ceremony induces the belief that the penalty will be exacted. Indeed, it is arguable

---

[7] Conceivably a sentencer might know that probation was felt by the offender as more severe than any other permissible penalty (at least one survey found that it was regarded by many English teenaged males as more to be feared than a fine). Or a sentencer might use it to express his view that the offender required treatment rather than retributive punishment. All I am suggesting is that there are cases in which a given type of sentence could *not* be justified on, say, retributive or expressive grounds.

[8] An exception is Sir Walter Moberly, who in *The Ethics of Punishment* (1968) seems to be arguing for all three, and to that extent was an eclectic.

that not even this is always necessary. Sentencing a murderer to life imprisonment, Thesiger J. said, 'In the past that act would have made you guilty of capital murder and you would have been sentenced to death'.[9] The suspended prison sentence, too, can be regarded as declaring, in effect, that the offence for which it is imposed is regarded with sufficient disapproval to call for, say, two years' imprisonment, without actually imposing it.[10]

By contrast, the retributive and the reductive justifications are genuine attempts to justify the actual imposition of penalties and not merely the creation of a belief that penalties are being imposed or are deserved. Moreover, the ceremonial denouncer must explain why such a belief should make the ceremony of sentencing satisfying; and, as I have said, the only plausible explanation is that it is satisfying to believers because they regard the penalties as retributively justified. In other words, a denouncer has to assume that those whom his penalties are meant to satisfy are retributivists.

Finally, if the denouncer believes that penalties have a beneficial effect upon people's moral attitudes — that is, if he is a reductive denouncer — he must admit that there is no empirical evidence to support him. On the contrary, it is only in special cases that the penalty for an individual offence receives national publicity. Some local newspapers report the sentences imposed in a few cases; but surveys do not suggest that these are noticed by many people. As for sentencing statistics, they seem to be studied by very few people indeed. I have been experimenting to see what effect penalties have on people's moral attitudes to selected types of offence, so far without finding any evidence that there is any such effect; but I am still trying.

A more credible kind of denouncer is the person who

[9] *Daily Telegraph,* 7 October 1977.
[10] The fact that it was intended by those who introduced it as an individual deterrent does not prevent denunciation-minded sentencers from using it in this way.

claims merely that the *offender's* attitude towards the offence is altered for the better by the symbolism of the penalty. Again there is no positive evidence for this; but at least it is certain that the symbol has been communicated to the person who is meant to be influenced. On the other hand, he is more likely than the public to regard the penalty as unjust, in which case the intended symbolic effect will not be achieved.

It is less easy to discredit reducers. The prevention of law-breaking — or as much of it as possible — has an obvious moral and pragmatic attraction. It is possible to criticise the over-enthusiastic reducer if he wants to penalise *all* infractions of the law however trivial; for this may antagonise people, and so forfeit their co-operation. It is also possible to argue that this law or that should not be enforced, perhaps because it seems a bad law. But neither of these criticisms would really undermine reductivism. More serious would be the argument — however far-fetched — that no laws should be enforced. If this is simply the anarchist's dogma that there should be no laws, it does not really touch the reducer, whose belief is that, given the existence of some good laws, efforts should be made to see that they are obeyed as often as possible. What should worry him, however, is a critic who agrees that laws are a good social institution, because they tell people how they should behave, but who also argues that to use penalties to enforce them is morally wrong. This critic might argue that the hardship which penalties generate is an evil. If so, the reductivist can only reply that it is outweighed by the greater evil prevented by law-enforcement.

Another objection to reductivism is that in its pure form it can lead to forms of enforcement which are unjust. Thus if one wants to maximise the deterrent effect of a penalty on a crime such as robbery, one should perhaps make sure that *someone* is penalised for every robbery, whether he is guilty of it or not. To this a pure but cynical reducer could reply that it would be counter-productive policy, since a system which was known to penalise at random would not deter,[11] and would antagonise the large number of people who believe in justice. Or, if he himself believed in justice, he could compromise with retributivism simply by agreeing that the innocent must not be penalised, even when this would improve the efficacy of law-enforcement. Similarly if he is attacked on the grounds that the protection of society or the reformation of offenders might call for periods of detention quite out of scale with what was retributively appropriate he could take either the cynical or the compromising way out.

There is a third line of argument, which merits mention, if not serious consideration. Rewarding conformity is sometimes said to be better than punishing law-breaking. 'Better' in this context usually means 'more likely to be effective', though it can also mean 'to some extent effective, but also avoiding undeserved harm'. There is, however, no evidence that it is more effective. Laboratory studies comparing the results of 'positive reinforcement' of behaviour by rewards with the results of 'negative reinforcement' by unpleasant stimuli tell us nothing about real life, in which the interval between behaviour and reward or penalty is a matter not of seconds or minutes but of weeks or months. It must of course be granted that rewards avoid undeserved harm: the only possible injustice is an undeserved or disproportionate reward. The objection to this argument is that a policy of rewarding virtue is impracticable. You cannot discredit reductivism by offering an alternative which is out of the question.

The most serious attack on the reducer is the argument that his methods do not work, so that he is inflicting evil in the form of penalties without achieving any countervailing prevention of future evil in the form of offences. In order to press this argument home it is necessary to produce evidence

---

[11] Or at best would deter only those who felt guilty over causing the innocent to be penalised.

contradicting the commonsense assumption that what is intended to deter deters and what is intended to reform reforms. There *is* a good deal of evidence suggesting that penalties which are intended to reform — such as probation or borstal training — seldom have this effect. The evidence for the inefficacy of deterrents, however, is very much scrappier and weaker, and at most supports the claim that the sorts of offences and the sorts of people who respond to deterrence are more restricted than the man in the street assumes (see Chapter 4). As for the protection of the public by incapacitation, it is very hard to argue that it is ineffective to execute an offender, or deport him or lock him up for a very long period. The most that can be argued is that in a society which no longer cares to use a capital punishment, can no longer transport its felons, and is no longer willing to lock sane people up until they die, the so-called protection of society means little more than the *postponement* of the offender's next offence (if indeed he is going to commit another). A substantial postponement, however, is not negligible: locking up a persistent robber for 10 years undoubtedly does reduce the total number of robberies which he commits, even if he takes up robbery again on release. More will be said about preventive sentences in Chapter 6.

The short answer, however, is that one cannot undermine the reducer by arguments about the ineffectiveness of penalties unless one is able to argue, with evidence, that penalties *never* reduce offences. It is not sufficient to argue that they seldom do, or that the evidence that they ever do is weak: one must be more or less certain that they never do.

Nevertheless, the reducer cannot ignore the argument that *most* of the penalties which are imposed in the hope of reducing the frequency of offences are not doing so. He is unable to distinguish between the cases in which penalties will have the desired effect and those in which they will not: at best he can make sensible guesses which will be right somewhat oftener than they would by chance. This is not a fatal objection. If he couples reductivism with distributive justice he can argue that so long as there is a substantial possibility of preventing more unhappiness for the innocent than he is inflicting on the culpable this is the proper choice. More practically, he might argue that even if we could distinguish the cases in which penalties would work from those in which they would not, it would be unwise to apply penalties in this selective way, since this would outrage people's sense of distributive justice, and so discredit the system. In any case, even a reducer who is thoroughly disillusioned about the effectiveness of attempts at individual deterrence or reformation can rely on another argument. If courts did not penalise the offenders whom they convicted, the police and other law enforcement agencies would take less trouble over their detection and prosecution, and the result of this would be an increase in the frequency of the offence in question. To justify penalties as an incentive for law-enforcers rather than a disincentive for offenders may seem cynical. But cynicism is not insincerity, and if the justifying aim is the prevention of as much crime as possible, within limits of the kind dictated by justice, the reducer can honestly argue this.

THE PROBLEMS OF RETRIBUTIVISM

Finally we come back to retributivism. Some objections to it are rational, some emotional. The emotional objections treat it as nothing more than a dignified form of vindictiveness. It is true that in practice it is sometimes difficult to be sure whether a sentencer is being genuinely retributive or giving vent to his sympathy with the victim. In theory, however, there is a clear distinction between reacting to injury or outrage and punishing *for the breach of a rule*. Only when the latter is the reason is the penalty genuine retributive punishment.

A more serious criticism is the difficulty which retributive sentencers feel, or ought to feel in deciding what kind and

amount of punishment corresponds to the culpability of this
or that offender. The decision involves two difficult feats of
estimation: the assessment of his culpability and the prediction of the amount of suffering which different punishments
will impose on him. It is much easier to say whether a man is
or is not culpable than to say exactly how culpable: even his
intimates can only guess at the strengths of the impulses,
temptations or pressures to which he was subject. As for how
much he will suffer from six months' or 12 months' imprisonment, or from a £100 fine, this is equally incalculable.
It is not surprising that some modern retributivists have
given up the hope of matching the quantum of punishment
to the culpability of the offender, and argue that their objective is not commensurability but mere proportionality:[12]
that is, the infliction of more severe punishments on the
more culpable offenders, together with the avoidance of
obvious inconsistencies (such as imprisoning one accomplice
and fining the other).

The most difficult question for the retributivist, however,
is 'Why *should* breaches of laws (or rules) be penalised?
Many moral philosophers have wrestled with this question,
and offered a variety of answers. Most of the answers fall
into one of three groups:

a. that punishment *purges* the offender's guilt by making him
suffer. Undoubtedly this is sometimes true as a psychological
statement. Some people feel guilty about some of the things
they do; and some of those who feel guilty feel less guilty if
they undergo suffering (voluntarily, accidentally or compulsorily) which they can in some way link to the offence. Moreover, there are also people who feel less censorious towards
an offender who has been made to suffer for an offence.
These, however, are mere psychological truths, and are not
even true about all offenders or all their condemners. They
do not alter the fact that an offender has acted culpably,

---

[12] For example, Sir Rupert Cross — following Hegel — argues this in
The English Sentencing System.

and they do not therefore satisfy those who want a non-psychological reason for retributive punishment, as distinct from a mere explanation.

b. that punishment induces repentance and other moral improvements in the offender. This should not be confused with the reductive aim of reform: it relies on moral improvement, not better behaviour. No doubt as a psychological statement it is sometimes true, just as it is sometimes true that suffering a penalty *lessens* feelings of guilt. One awkward question is whether it is true often enough to make it reasonable to hope for an induced repentance. But if it is granted that a reducer can be discredited only by showing that he *never* achieves his aims, the same concession must be made to this kind of punisher. A much more awkward question is whether he would regard as punishment a penalty inflicted on an offender who is known to be incapable of moral improvement (supposing such certainty to be possible). Sir Walter Moberly, who includes this amongst his explanations of the virtues of punishment, does not go as far as to say that in such a case a penalty could not be justified.[13] On the whole such a view does not seem to correspond with what is usually meant by retribution.

c. that punishment is an effort to *cancel* the offence: to bring about a state of affairs in which it is as if it had not been committed. This is sometimes possible. A thief who has stolen money can sometimes be made to return it; and unless the owner was beggared by the theft he is no worse off. A vandal can be made to pay for the restoration of what he has damaged; and if it is not an irreparable work of art nobody else suffers. Such situations, however, are rare. Even if the loss or damage is of a kind which is capable of being put right, the offender usually lacks the means to do so. (State compensation is a more effective way of restoring

[13] See his *The Ethics of Punishment.* But his great-niece, Dr. E. S. Moberly, seems to go to this length in her book *Suffering, Innocent and Guilty.*

the *status quo ante* where this is at all possible: but that is not punishing the offender.) In fact, we tend to *distinguish* between penalty and restitution. This being so, in what sense does a fine or a prison sentence *cancel* the offence? Only in some non-literal sense. For example, a society might regard the doing of wrong to a wrongdoer as a *symbol* of the cancellation which they would have liked to achieve in reality.[14] If this is what is being argued, it belongs to the expressive justification rather than the retributive; for the symbolic function would be adequately performed if people believed that the offender had been punished, whether he had in fact been or not.

d. that punishment is *deserved* by the offender. Philosophers, however, do not find it easy to explain what is meant by 'deserving'. It has even been suggested that a desert is 'a right'; but a right is something that one claims or not, as one wishes, and it is only in special circumstances that offenders claim the right to be punished.[15] More plausible is the suggestion that offenders have *forfeited* a right, variously defined as the right not to be deliberately made to suffer, or the right to one's liberty and property. It does not much matter how the right is defined; for the notion of a forfeited right cannot provide the positive justification for punishing which the retributivist needs. The notion of desert seems to involve the belief that a person who has acted culpably should suffer for his action, and that unpunished wrong-doing is somehow a greater evil than punished wrong-doing.

A satisfactory retributive answer to the question, 'Why should offences be punished?' has to meet a number of requirements:

(i) it must make retribution clearly distinguishable from mere vengeance or denunciation;

---

[14] This is what Bosanquet seems to be saying.

[15] *e.g.*, when they feel very guilty, or fear lynching, or are faced with some other unpleasant alternative, such as indefinite detention in a mental hospital: see p. 46.

(ii) it must allow penalties to be proportional to rather than commensurate with culpability;

(iii) it must account psychologically for the retributivist's feeling that unpunished wrongdoing is a greater evil than punished wrongdoing (without implying that it is *sufficient* to explain it psychologically);

(iv) it must make punishment not permissible but obligatory (in the absence of excuses). If it made it merely permissible some other positive justification for it would have to be found; and if the retributive answer did not supply this it would follow that the answer must be non-retributive.

Some people would also argue that:

(v) the answer must also make it clear why the natural or accidental consequences of wrongdoing are not punishment. If, for example, a burglar is injured by barbed wire or by an outraged householder, is his injury distinguishable from punishment? If so, is this reconcilable with the fact that even a retributively minded sentencer might well lighten his sentence because of the injury he had suffered?[16] Some people feel that guilt is partially — or even wholly — purged by suffering which is the natural or accidental result of the wrongdoing. More will be said about 'natural punishment' in Chapter 6.

Only one answer seems to meet all these points: that *retributive punishment is a penalty imposed in fulfilment of a requirement in a rule that it should be imposed on those who have infringed a rule*. As has already been said, this is what distinguishes it from mere vengeance, which is inflicted for emotional reasons. It also distinguishes it from denunciation, which requires only the belief that the offender will suffer the penalty. It allows the penalty to be proportional rather than commensurate to culpability; for the rule need not insist

---

[16] This sometimes happens in the case of motoring offenders who have been responsible for the death or injury of someone dear to them.

on commensurability. It provides a psychological explanation of the feeling that an unpunished infringement is worse than a punished one. Man is a rule-making, rule-following animal, and most of his activities — linguistic, social, recreational and sexual — are governed by rules or conventions. There is nothing like conforming with a rule for inducing a feeling of propriety or even righteousness. An unpunished infraction means two infractions.

As for the requirement that the explanation should also make punishment obligatory, this is met if the rule dealing with punishment is mandatory, but not if it makes it merely permissive. Mandatory punishments can still be found in most penal codes, especially for certain kinds of murder;[17] and in the past some penal codes made certain punishments (or minimum punishments) obligatory for quite a range of offences, even if in practice courts found ways round the obligation when they wanted to. The fact that in codes of the modern type most penalties are not mandatory but merely permissive is not an objection. All it means is that such codes are not retributive, except in so far as they limit the severity of penalties and confine them to guilty persons. If a penalty is merely permitted by a code, a sentencer must have some non-retributive justification for choosing to impose it, whether reductive or expressive. It is true that a judge who is sentencing someone under the code may reason retributively even when choosing a permissible sentence; but if he does he is following some private rule which tells him that it is correct to punish.

The rule-answer, however, is not without problems. Suppose that the aim of the legislators who drew up the penal code was not retributive but reductive (or expressive); and that they made penalties mandatory in order to maxi-mise deterrence (or denunciation). Would this mean that sentences imposed under the code would be non-retributive?

[17] A more humdrum example is mandatory disqualification from driving a car as a result of certain convictions.

This re-emphasises the confusion which arises from talking about 'the' aim, reason or justification for a penalty, instead of distinguishing the aim (etc.) of the legislator, the sentencer and the penal agent who carries out the sentence. The aim of a legislator may be non-retributive; but if the sentencer imposes a penalty because he regards himself as bound to do so either by the law he is administering or by some unwritten rule, then according to the rule-theory he is sentencing retributively. But could a legislator then have retributive reasons for drawing up a mandatory code of penalties? Yes, if he did so because he was following a *moral* rule that wrong-doing should be penalised.

If we turn to codes which are completely silent about penalties must we then say that people who are intentionally made to suffer for breaches of them are not being retributively punished? This certainly seems to be what we feel about breaches of good manners: they incur dislike, perhaps even retaliation, but not what we call punishment. On the other hand, parents are said to punish children, though families seldom have explicit mandatory penalties. The rule-theory would say that if parents rightly claim to be punishing retributively they must have made it clear to their children that certain kinds of behaviour will, unless excusable, incur some penalty.

One important feature of the rule-theory is that it poses a very serious difficulty for the eclectic sentencer. If the positive justification for imposing a penalty in a given case is that the rules require it, so that to refrain from doing so is to add one infraction to another, can the eclectic reconcile this with a decision to sentence in certain types of case in accordance with, say, reductive aims? Only if the rules say that he can make exceptions, or if he is willing to breach a rule that requires a penalty. Otherwise, the eclectic must be following a private set of rules which sometimes coincide with the official rules and sometimes do not. In cruder terms, one cannot justify retributive punishment on the grounds that it is dictated by the rules if one is prepared to ignore that dictate when one thinks best.

To sum up:

1. The denouncer is either a crypto-reducer or a quasi-punisher. He is the former if he believes that sentences educate the public morally. He is the latter if he regards sentences as ceremonials which give satisfaction, since without retributive feelings there would be no satisfaction. Denunciation is thus not an independent justification.

2. The reducer cannot be discredited completely. It can be shown that he is causing a lot of unhappiness by inflicting penalties of which only an unknown but probably small fraction is having the desired effect. It can also be argued that the more drastic of the reductive techniques are morally objectionable. But on his own ground he cannot be completely floored.

3. Nor can the punisher be thoroughly discredited. At most it can be argued that his answer to the question 'Why should wrongdoing be punished?' namely, 'Because the rules say so,' is a rather formal one, even if it does meet the criteria for an adequate answer. It can also be pointed out that in modern penal codes almost all penalties are permissible, not obligatory, so that a sentencer who claims to be punishing on retributive grounds must be obeying some extra-legal rule.

Where does this leave the eclectic who regards himself as free to choose between justifications according to the circumstances of each case? He is not being illogical so long as he can rationally and plausibly distinguish between the circumstances in which he appeals to each of his repertoire of justifications, or alternatively can show that he is consistently following a set of priorities, and not merely choosing emotionally because he feels indignation or sympathy.

This means that he must certainly be more careful than most sentencers are in practice when justifying their sentences. He must be especially careful when using the expressive justification to be clear what he means; and unless he means that he is educating people[18] he should think twice about using it at all. When he wants to appeal to the retributive justification he should ask himself whether the law compels him to punish; and if − as in most cases − it does not (but merely allows it) he should realise that the rule he is following is a private one. When he wants to justify his sentence on utilitarian grounds he should ask himself whether in the particular case before him his sentence has any chance of being effective, or whether he is imposing it simply in order to maintain the consistency and credibility of the system. His hardest problem is to produce a respectable distinction − that is, one that is more than a mere emotional reaction − between the cases in which he appeals to retribution and those in which he appeals to utility. Probably the best he can do is to say, 'This is a case in which my private rules require punishment (or do not, as the case may be)'. One thing is certain: eclecticism does not escape the difficulties of any of the different justifications between which it oscillates.

The choice seems to lie between a rather formal version of retributivism, a distinctly pessimistic reductivism and an eclecticism which has not yet rationalised its principles of selection.

[18] Even when this is what he means he should ask himself such obvious questions as, 'Will this sentence receive any publicity?'. There is also the question, 'Do even well-publicised sentences really affect people's moral attitudes towards the offences for which they are imposed, as distinct from their fear of the penalties?'. This can be answered only by carefully conducted research, of a kind which I have been carrying out, so far with negative results.

3 Treating

The treatment of offenders has been the subject of several discoveries in recent years. Lawyers in the U.S.A. have discovered a right[1] to treatment, at least when one is committed compulsorily to a mental hospital or a juvenile reformatory. Penologists have discovered the ineffectiveness of treatment, including reformatory treatment. This has led to the discovery of the right to be punished instead, especially when this means getting out earlier. Moralists have discovered C.S. Lewis' objections — and some new ones — even to treatment that does work, if of course there is such a thing.

Can one really talk in this general way about the wide assortment of expedients employed in dealing with offenders? Have they enough in common?

To a certain extent they share the aim of altering behaviour so that it is more acceptable to other members of the society.[2] Sometimes the aim is limited to promoting law-abiding behaviour: sometimes it is more ambitious, and includes the improvement of the offender as a husband, father, worker. In the case of psychiatric treatment it may even be to make him happier. To qualify as 'treatment' the expedient must rely on something more than threats or inducements, and something more than mere incapacitation. To qualify as even the mildest of successes it must produce

---

[1] The nature of rights, and especially offenders' rights, is the subject of Chapter 8.

[2] Some conflict-theorists would say 'acceptable to those groups in a society who wield power through the penal system'. Admittedly such groups set more rigid — and in some cases silly — standards of behaviour. But even the powerless dislike being killed, robbed or raped.

some alteration in the offender so that even when presented with tempting opportunities to repeat his offence he does so less often than he would have. Finally, the alteration must not be too transient: it must last longer than a pill.

COMPULSION

What are the anti-treaters objecting to? In some discussions it is the *compulsory* doing of certain things to people in the name of sentencing, or psychiatry or social work, as the case may be:

> To be cured against one's will (wrote C. S. Lewis a quarter of a century ago) and cured of states which we may not regard as disease is to be put on a level with those who have not yet reached the age of reason or those who never will; to be classed with infants, imbeciles and domestic animals. But to be punished, however severely, because we have deserved it ... is to be treated as a human person made in God's image.

Lewis' splendid rhetoric may blind us to one or two points. First, if he admits, as he seems to, that where compulsory treatment is concerned we can justifiably claim to know better than children, imbeciles and animals, why does he draw the line exactly there? What he does not discuss is the problems posed by three kinds of case:

a) the adult non-imbecile whose condition or behaviour is making *him* unhappy, but who refuses treatment because of some prejudice or ungrounded fear. Are we not to be allowed to say that although he is a non-subnormal adult whose other views and decisions we respect, whether we agree with them or not, he is in this respect behaving irrationally and against his own interest? Are we never allowed to 'know better' than someone simply because he is adult? To say 'never' seems to imply that knowing better derogates from his adult status even when it is limited to some very specific decision.

b) the adult non-imbecile who resists proposals for treatment because his condition or behaviour, though it harms or grieves others, does not make *him* unhappy? Since what we are considering is the ethics of compulsorily treating such a person we are entitled to say to Lewis 'Suppose that we have a choice between imposing on such a person effective treatment that will not make him unhappy — or not for very long — and the alternative of punishing him again and again according to his deserts (or leaving him to God to punish if what he is doing is a sin but not a criminal offence). Which would you choose?'. Lewis is then in an awkward position. He must either stand fast, and say 'Punishment every time', or embark on a discussion of the exact nature of the harm or grief that the man is causing, and the exact effects of the treatment. Is the grief due simply to prejudice — for example on the part of parents who want their son treated for homosexuality — or is it what might be called 'natural' grief? Has the treatment injurious side-effects, such as stigma or some psychological disability? If Lewis consented to discuss such matters he would compromise his position. He must, I think, say 'Punishment every time'. And if he does he must explain how he can draw so sharp a distinction between adults and children, imbeciles and non-imbeciles. In the end, it seems to me, he must either compromise or go further than he does — that is, must argue that not even in the case of children and imbeciles are we justified in compulsory treatment. And if he argues this about children, he must then either forbid us to do what we call 'bringing them up properly' or else define 'treatment' so narrowly as to exclude that sort of thing.

c) Lewis' third unacknowledged problem is the sane adult who has done serious harm to someone else and if left to himself is likely to do it again. It is true that there are fewer such people than is popularly supposed, and that placing someone in that category must always involve a certain amount of over-prediction.[3] But unless Lewis tells us that we must never think in terms of future danger to others he is faced with an awkward choice when such a person refuses treatment. Either he must be set free after serving no more than his just sentence for what he has so far done, or he must be detained until long incarceration renders him harmless, probably by destroying part of what Lewis would call his humanity.[4]

CONSENT

The objectors to compulsory treatment are usually also worried, and with reason, about the question 'What constitutes valid consent?'. We know of course that the notion of consent raises problems where children are concerned; but even in the case of adults there are difficulties. In the case of physical treatment it is usually regarded as a prerequisite of genuine consent that the patient

1) understands the nature of the treatment, with its attendant risks, discomforts and likelihood of success;
2) is not under some sort of coercion.

These prerequisites, however, raise difficulties where the inmates of mental hospitals or prisons are concerned. Patients may be unable to understand the nature of what is being offered; or their judgement may be impaired, as in the case of severe depression.[5] Even the National Council for Civil

---

[3] See Chapter 5.

[4] If he changes his mind during his incarceration, and consents to treatment, he raises moral questions which I discuss later.

[5] According to a report in the *New Scientist* for 26 February 1976 it has even been ruled (by a Michigan court) that lack of knowledge about the great risks and unproven efficacy of psychosurgery make informed consent to it virtually impossible.

Liberties conceded, in their evidence to the Butler Committee, that treatment without consent would be justifiable in
the case of emergency procedures, for example to curtail
sudden outbursts of violence or relieve acute depressive
states. The Butler Committee's conclusion was that the
basic rule should be that treatment (other than nursing care)
should not be imposed without the patient's consent if he
is able to appreciate what is involved, but with three exceptions: if it represented the minimum interference necessary
to prevent violent or dangerous behaviour on the spot; if it
is necessary to save his life; or if it is needed to prevent him
from deteriorating. And if he cannot appreciate what is
involved, treatment can be imposed without consent, but
only after a second opinion if irreversible procedures are
involved. As a member of the Committee I am bound to
regard this as a reasonable solution.

When it comes to prisoners, the problem is not usually
inability to understand what is involved, but the extent to
which the prisoner is under some sort of coercion. Here
people often fail to think clearly, and argue that if the
choice is between treatment with a possibility of earlier
release and no treatment with no possibility of earlier release the choice is not a free one and the consent is therefore
not real. This is muddled. A choice is none the less real or
rational simply because one of the alternatives is more
attractive: otherwise most choices would be unreal.

The most that can be argued is that it is morally wrong
to *offer* a prisoner this sort of choice. Even this takes some
justifying. If we grant for the sake of argument that the penal
system has a right to detain him for the period of his sentence, why should it not release him earlier if he chooses and
responds to treatment? There are two possible arguments:
   1) that his sentence represents the right amount of punish-
      ment from a retributive point of view, and should not
      therefore be diminished simply because he is less likely
      to offend again.
Only a punisher of the old-fashioned, Kantian, kind can argue

this; and few of those who object to the sort of choice we are discussing are Kantians. A more sophisticated argument of the same kind is that it is unfair to release X earlier than Y simply because X by a happy chance — not through repentance or any other virtuous act — is more responsive to treatment than Y. But since we have no qualms about doing just this with non-offenders in hospitals, the objection to doing the same with prisoners must again be old-fashioned retributivism.

2) that neither the treaters nor anyone else can tell whether the prisoner is really responding to treatment, assuming for the moment that some prisoners do respond.

This may be an overstated cliché, but it has enough truth in it to force us to consider our present sentencing system. In the first place, one of the main reasons why it is so hard to assess response is that it cannot be assessed in conditions of captivity. The solution to this difficulty, however, is not necessarily to abandon assessment; it may be to grant freedom leave from prisons or hospitals with much more liberality and in graduated stages. With all its defects and critics, the parole system is a step in this direction.

INDETERMINACY

The second trouble, however, is that the treatment ideology is assumed to be indissolubly linked to indeterminacy in the length of sentence. 'The first result' wrote Lewis 'of the Humanitarian theory is ... to substitute for a definite sentence ... an indefinite sentence terminable only by the word of those experts ... who inflict it' (ibid. 226). As an historical statement this is nonsense. Truly indeterminate sentences, such as 'life', are the creation not of a treatment ideology but of a desire either to inflict the supreme punishment short of death or to protect the public from offenders who are supposed to be especially dangerous. It is *semi*-determinate sentences, with the possibility of release between fixed minima and maxima, for which the idea of penal treatment is responsible: an example is the borstal sentence. In the British system, however, the treatment ideology cannot really be blamed for a lot of semi-determinacy. Remission is quite independent of any notion of response to treatment, and even parole is largely linked with estimates of the risk involved in release, which are based much more on factors such as the prisoner's record and the situation in which he will find himself on release than on assessments of his response to treatment, if any.

My main point, however, is that there *is* no indissoluble logical link between the notion of treatment and indeterminacy or even semi-determinacy. There is no reason why someone who believes in treatment should not say to a would-be treater 'If you think your treatment will do this offender any good, you can have him — subject to his consent — for the time allowed by the sentencing tariff. If you find you need longer, *he* will have to consent to an extension'. If the would-be treater complained that the tariff sentence was too short for his purposes, I would ask him for evidence that a longer period was likely to be more effective: a request that he would have difficulty in meeting.

As for those who are bothered by the difficulty of telling whether X has responded better than Y, or by the inequity of letting him out earlier simply because he is lucky enough to be more responsive, the solution is to say to the prisoner 'You are offered such and such a form of treatment. You can refuse it without any fear of being kept longer than your sentence allows or of being dealt with more harshly. But if you accept it and co-operate in it your sentence will be shortened by so much, *whether the treatment seems to be doing you any good or not.*'

It is arguable that this is still what has been called a 'coerced choice'; that is, between alternatives of which one is unthinkable for any sensible person. This has more force if one of the alternatives is really dreadful such as death or lifelong incarceration, than if it is simply a slightly longer period of detention. After all, quite a number of perfectly sane prisoners — especially in Scotland — have refused parole and chosen to wait for their remission. A choice is really objectionable on such grounds only if one alternative is either morally unjustifiable or artificially devised with the object of creating an illusion of choice. But those who are still troubled *could* go one step further, and simply offer the prisoner the choice between doing his time with or without treatment.

SPURIOUSNESS

Sometimes, however, the target of criticism is not compulsory treatment but the unfulfilled promise of treatment. In the U.S.A. there have been successful appeals against commitment to mental hospitals and juvenile institutions on the grounds that these commitments were for treatment which the hospitals or institutions were not in fact providing.

An appeal of this kind would be unlikely to succeed in Britain, at least so far as compulsory admission to mental hospitals is concerned. The draftsmen of the Mental Health Act 1959 were careful to define 'medical treatment' as including not only nursing but also 'care and training under medical supervision'. In other words, so long as the patient gets some nursing or care or training, and so long as there is a doctor around, he cannot argue that he is not getting the treatment for which he was compulsorily admitted. This seems to me defensible. His condition might be of a kind that cannot be improved by any known technique; yet he might be happier in a mental hospital than in prison or at large in society.[6]

[6] Let us get a distraction out of the way: the case of the patient or inmate who frustrates attempts at treatment by being unco-operative. Presumably he forfeits the right to appeal on the grounds I have defined, although he will pop up again later when I come to consider the objections to *effective* treatment.

This is not an attempt to dodge the main question. First of all, an ambiguous definition of treatment is itself objectionable if it deprives a person of the right of arguing a *prima facie* case by adopting criteria so wide that hardly anything could fail to satisfy them. In Britain nothing but a prolonged and total strike of medical and nursing staff would enable a mental hospital patient to argue that he was not getting treatment. At the very least it ought to be made clear in each case whether the patient is being put inside with the hope of improving his condition or behaviour, or with some less ambitious aim. Second, whatever the legal position in the jurisdiction in which he happens to be, it is arguable that a person *should* have the chance of a successful appeal on the grounds that he was subjected to loss of freedom of a particular kind on the assumption that this would make possible an attempt to improve his condition or behaviour by some technique or other, and that in fact no such technique is being applied to him. Such appeals in the U.S.A. have led to marked improvements in institutional regimes.

INEFFECTIVENESS

This brings us, however, to the next target for criticism: that most or all the kinds of treatment on offer are ineffective.

Here penal treatment seems to have arrived at the same position as psychotherapy, although rather later. Very few properly controlled trials support the belief that either is effective; but both continue to be practised. In fairness, however, several points must be made:
1) in most reported trials there was little or no effort to select, for treatment and control samples, subjects who were *prima facie* likely to respond. One of the few experiments in which this was done — called the PICO project — did show differences in recidivism between bright, verbal and anxious young males who received psychotherapy, and bright, verbal and anxious ones

who did not.[7]

2) most of the studies reviewed — by Rachman for psychotherapy and Martinson for penal treatment — were
dismissed because of faulty methodology.[8]

3) where the methodology was acceptable we are usually
told simply that there was no significant difference
between treated and control samples. But in many cases
the samples were so small that only a very large difference would have reached an acceptable level of
significance.

4) in most of the sounder trials of penal treatment it was
carried out far from thoroughly or under conditions
that were far from ideal: under considerable deprivation
of liberty, artificial living conditions and by staff who
had neither been selected nor trained with a view to
the treatment in question. A dismal illustration is
Kassebaum's report of a group counselling experiment
in a Californian prison.[9]

In any case, so far as offenders are concerned, the evidence
does not demonstrate what most people think it does: that
treatment does not work. It is hardly ever possible to compare the effect of treatment with the effect of doing nothing
to an offender; so that most studies are assessments of comparative, not absolute, efficacy: they compare the effect of,
say, ordinary imprisonment with the effect of some improvement on imprisonment. When they find that this makes no
difference to the reconviction-rate, this does not mean that
neither are effective: only that the improvement is no more
effective. Moreover, as has been said, there is always the possibility that if we knew how to identify those suitable for
treatment we could do better. The evidence does not justify
abandoning such efforts, or the search for new techniques.

[7] See S. Adams 'The PICO Project' (1961).
[8] See S. Rachman *The Effects of Psychotherapy* and R. Martinson's
'What Works?' in *The Public Interest*.
[9] See G. Kassebaum *et al.*, *Prison Treatment and Parole Survival*.

INHUMANITY AND DEGRADATION

The fourth kind of treatment to which people object is *inhumane* treatment. No matter whether it is both voluntary and effective: if it is inhumane it is condemned. Article 3 of the European Convention on Human Rights stipulates that 'no-one shall be subjected to ... inhuman or degrading treatment ... ' but it does not define inhumanity or degradation. Sometimes what people have in mind is the infliction of suffering. But to be inhumane suffering has to be inflicted unnecessarily and callously, or with enjoyment. If it is inseparable from effective treatment, and if the patient has been warned of it and has given a genuine consent, it can hardly be called inhumane.

What about degradation? This seems to involve the notion of something more than mere humiliation; for so many kinds of sentence, and even conviction itself, are humiliating. It must mean demotion from some sort of grade or status. What sort of status? Hardly that which the person *happens* to have attained, or else any penalty that derogated from that status would be prohibited, and we should not be allowed to disqualify drivers, teachers or company directors. The status must presumably be something common to everyone: that of being human. If so, degradation is a very difficult criterion to apply in practice. If a patient is made to vomit under aversion therapy is he being degraded? And what if he is not conscious of the spectacle that he is providing – that is, if he himself does not *feel* degraded?

It would be more sensible to say that what is meant is that the *result* of the treatment must not be the irreversible dehumanisation of the person.[10,11] Then the focus of concern

[10] Presumably it would not matter whether the result was intended or merely a probable side-effect.

[11] Those who object to degradation, of course, may find themselves in an uncomfortable position when asked what they would do about so-called 'human vegetables' who are kept alive only by elaborate techniques. It is true that they can make a distinction between the results of accidents and the unwanted results of therapeutic efforts, but the distinction is a fairly fine one.

would be procedures such as castration, leucotomy and institutionalisation. Castration is a good example, because there is no doubt that some people object to the use of it even when it is voluntary and successful in its aim.

Some people carry this line of argument further, and object to voluntary effective treatment which does not render the subject subhuman but substantially alters his personality. It is not easy to find an unequivocal statement of this point of view; but Nicholas Kittrie seems to be expressing it in *The Right to be Different.* Certainly he talks of the need to preserve 'human variation and pluralism', and makes several suggestions. Among them are

1) that certain surgical, chemical or psychological techniques be outlawed altogether; and/or
2) that 'one might attempt to delineate personality characteristics that would be immune from alteration', and/or
3) that 'perhaps the propriety of treatment should depend on whether the treatment is constituted for the benefit of the patient as an end in himself rather than as a means to broader social aims'.

Unfortunately, Kittrie does not give examples. Presumably the surgical, chemical and psychological techniques that he would ban are those that he regards as inhuman or degrading; but he does not say. Again, to what sort of personality characteristics would he grant immunity? Suppose that someone finds that his misplaced sense of humour or tendency to be generous beyond his means is getting him into trouble, would Kittrie forbid him to seek help? One writer, the anti-psychiatrist David Cooper, goes as far as to say that neither frigidity nor premature ejaculation should be regarded as matters for treatment. It would be unfair to foist this example onto Kittrie; but it is important to see how far this line of argument can be carried.

It is Kittrie's other suggestion, however, that is most interesting: the rule that the treatment must be for the benefit of the patient himself and not simply a means to broader social aims. Suppose that we have a patient who enjoys gambling, but has a conscience and realises that he is causing his family intolerable anxieties. If he asks for a cure should it be refused on the grounds that this is a broader social aim? Should a psychiatrist offer to cure his guilt rather than his gambling? Surely that would also be treatment. But to refuse to treat either would be to leave the man to suffer from his conflict.

Such points of view are too often stated in the form of self-evident truths with their own built-in appeal to liberal sentiment. Sometimes they are supported, however, by the argument that treating behaviour involves imposing values that have no moral authority. Whichever form it takes, the personality is accorded some sort of immunity from interference, rather like the goings-on inside embassies. Nor is it clear whether the immunity applies to *unofficial* attempts to change character, for example when parents are bringing up children. If we are talking of 'rights' this is no mere sophistry. If parents have a right to do this why not other lawful authorities? Or is it again a matter of age? If on the other hand we regard parents as having to act from necessity and without a right, can it be maintained that there are no other circumstances in which this necessity arises — for example, in the case of serious law-breaking?

One more point. The opponents of treatment are fond of the argument that it is based on an inappropriate medical model. Yet they too are falling into the same error when they assume that treatment *must* mean suffering or degradation. It suits their case; but it is fair to ask first whether this is true of all genuine medical treatment — and of course it isn't — and second whether it need be true of psychiatric or penal treatment. Grendon is regarded by most prisoners to whom I have talked as a good deal *less* unpleasant than ordinary prisons. The Clockwork Orange was nasty, but after all it wasn't a real orange.

Having said all this, I must admit that we may soon reach a stage at which we shall have to consider what a penal system would be like if the treatment ideology had to be abandoned completely. This may sound a wholly academic notion, but what I said at the outset about the policies of treatment in Scandinavia and the U.S.A. should have emphasised that it is a live, practical issue.

THE ELIMINATION OF TREATMENT

To talk, however, of eliminating treatment — or any other penal aim — is an oversimplification. Whatever aims a government or a legislature may have in mind (and it would be remarkable if every member of it shared the same penal philosophy) these cannot automatically dictate the aims of sentencers, who in turn cannot dictate the aims of those who carry out sentences. In Britain, for example, preventive detention was expressly provided for nothing more than the protection of the public against offenders who were supposed to be beyond reform; yet it came to be regarded as laying an obligation on prisons to attempt to treat these very offenders, so that preventive detention was criticised for the high reconviction-rates of released detainees who were supposed to be selected for this incorrigibility.

Still, if the prisons could be publicly released from the Gladstonian duty to attempt reform, they could respond with less spiritual difficulty than could other agencies, partly because they have other competing objectives — such as security — partly because only a few penal establishments are deeply committed to the idea of treatment. Other aims on which they could then concentrate more wholeheartedly and with more optimism are (not in any order of merit)
  a) the alleviation of unwanted side-effects of custody, such as institutionalisation and estrangement from families;
  b) tackling problems of a kind that are remediable, such as ill-health or illiteracy;
  c) reducing the cost of imprisonment, for example by making prison work efficient rather than trying to suit the prisoner's need.

TREATMENT IN THE OPEN

The probation and after-care services would be in a greater difficulty. Admittedly a great deal of their work consists of practical assistance rather than treatment. To tell a probation officer, however, that he can find an offender a good job and nice lodgings but must not try to alter his attitude to work is like telling him to teach someone to swim without tackling his fear of the water. And is he allowed to reason with the probationer, to point out to him where his long-term interest lies? Is an effort to induce him to behave more rationally[1 2] an effort to alter his character? Are non-directive techniques of counselling as objectionable as directive ones?

TREATMENT AND THE OFFENDER

Again, what about the offender's point of view? Suppose he says, as some offenders do, 'I want to be cured, and am willing to undergo whatever treatment will cure me'. Is he to be told that the chances of cure are so small as to rule this out, or that he can seek treatment on his own, after his release or independently of his probation or the payment of his fine? It is true that some offenders' demands for treatment are their way of shifting responsibility onto society; but some demands are genuine. Would not a reply of that kind make them more pessimistic about their chances of keeping out of trouble, and even more cynical about the *bona fides* of the system?

OUTLAWING TREATMENT

And how is the outlawing of treatment to be managed? A

[1 2] I am not begging the question as to whether the offender's offence may or may not have been rational conduct, given his goals and values. Whatever they are, it is possible to discuss with him which have priority and what behaviour is likely to achieve them.

certain amount can no doubt be achieved in a hierarchical organisation such as the prison service simply by an obvious waning of enthusiasm or a change of governor: that is what happened to group counselling in Britain. Treatment of a kind that needs resources can be starved of them. But to go further and forbid penal agents, whether prison or probation staff, to take even the most obvious opportunities for altering the attitudes of offenders to their social environment would be seen as intolerable regimentation, especially by probation officers and other social workers, to say nothing of the effect which it would have on recruitment. What sort of person is going to apply for a job of that kind?

This being so, treatment would have to be discredited rather than forbidden or discouraged. The media of discredit would presumably include articles and talks by penal reformers who were prepared to be sufficiently sweeping in their denunciations: those who insisted on analysing the evidence and the ideological arguments would be less persuasive. Preservice and in-service training could be used to de-doctrinate new entrants – but only when the teachers had been dedoctrinated or replaced by re-indoctrinated successors: a slow process. Nevertheless, it is already beginning.

TREATMENT AND SENTENCING

Sentencing presents a different problem. It would in theory be possible, by statute or by decisions of appellate courts, to rule out the alteration of an offender's character as a legitimate consideration in sentencing; so that, for example, it would no longer be proper to impose a prison sentence, or increase it,[13] simply in order to allow enough time for a course of treatment. Tariff-sentencing – whether based on retributive, denunciatory or deterrent considerations –

---

[13] As *R. v. Turner* (1967) 51 Cr. App. R., 72, allowed English courts to do.

would probably become even commoner than at present. Not all 'individualised' sentences,[14] however, would be ruled out. If *culpability* were the governing consideration, factors that mitigated this could be taken into account. If individual *deterrence* were the consideration, any reasonable ground for thinking that the offender was unlikely to repeat his offence could be allowed to reduce the severity of the sentence. Again, the *protection of others* would sometimes justify a longer, or different, sentence. All that would be ruled out would be individualisation for the sake of treatment.

A major problem would of course arise as soon as it was conceded that exceptions could be made to the 'no treatment' rule; and an obvious candidate would be the mentally disordered offender, partly because of the feeling that he may not have been fully responsible, partly because of a greater optimism — whether justified or not — about treatment in such cases.[15] If we make this concession, why not others? What about the immature offender? Here again we have a vague feeling that he is not fully responsible, although it gets vaguer the higher legislators raise the critical age. Most teenagers know the nature and quality of their doings, know when they are illegal and have sufficient self-control to wait until there are no adults about. But is the responsibility issue really relevant to treatment? We can regard someone as not responsible even if we regard him as not treatable. The case for making an exception to the 'no treatment' rule for juveniles must rest on optimism about treatment; and this has taken some hard knocks of late, especially where residential treatment is concerned.[16]

[14] See D. A. Thomas *Principles of Sentencing*.

[15] It is also arguable that if we do not deny prisoners treatment for physical disorders we should not deny them treatment for mental ones. But that is not a sentencing consideration, since psychiatric treatment can be arranged for prisoners.

[16] See the discouraging review of results in D.B. Cornish and R.V.G. Clarke's *Residential Treatment and Its Effects on Delinquency*.

Irrespective, however, of the number of candles on one's birthday-cake, should it be possible to argue in occasional cases that a sane offender should be an exception to the 'no treatment' rule? We might perhaps concede this, subject to several stipulations, such as

1) that he must consent;
2) that it must not involve greater restriction on his freedom than that to which he would have been subject if sentenced ordinarily;
3) that the resources for treatment already exist and do not have to be provided at considerable cost for a small number of offenders;
4) that the prospects of success really are substantial.

How often these conditions would be fulfilled I cannot say; certainly not with embarrassing frequency.

CONCLUSION

To sum up, I have tried to drive home three points. First that the discrediting of treatment is of more than academic importance, whether for the penal system or for psychiatry. Second, that it owes its appeal to a mixture of accusations — compulsion, pseudo-consent, indeterminacy in sentencing, spuriousness, ineffectiveness, inhumanity, degradation, interference with the integrity of the personality — not all of which can be levelled at all kinds of treatment but all of which can be assembled into an intellectual blunderbuss. There *are* dangers in the treatment ideology, but they are more likely to be avoided if they are clearly distinguished. Third, that any attempt to eliminate treatment from penal systems — let alone mental hospitals — must overcome great difficulties, not least of which would be the hopes of both staff and offenders.

What is valuable, however, is *scepticism* about treatment if it makes us ask the right question. Is what we are doing really treatment or simply smooth management? If it *is* treatment, what evidence is there for its efficacy? If it *is* effective, at what cost in terms of resources and suffering? So long as these questions are asked and answered we should not abandon all efforts to devise effective forms of treatment.

4 Deterring

Why is deterrence, one of the oldest techniques of social control, nowadays so discreditable? Partly because it is associated in people's minds with inhumane kinds of penalty, and especially capital punishment. Deterrence is, after all, the *deliberate* threat of harm with the purpose of discouraging specified types of conduct: a threat which, if it is to be credible, has to be carried out. In a non-sadistic culture the deliberate infliction of death, pain or other harm is seen as requiring a very strong justification if it is not to be condemned. Dentists and surgeons, who knowingly cause pain, are tolerated only because they are believed to be conferring a benefit which outweighs the pain. If the benefit is doubtful or non-existent, toleration very quickly turns into censure. Or if the benefit excludes the person harmed, this too is nowadays regarded by many people as morally unacceptable. It is all right, even praiseworthy, if someone decides to die for his country; but no longer all right to compel him to do so against his will.

Both these arguments are well-known objections to deterrents. More recently I have heard a political argument. Although I cannot find it in the literature, it was put forward in discussion at the Stockholm Symposium on deterrence in 1975. It is that deterrents are used only to maintain the political *status quo*. This implies of course that the *status quo* is bound to be worse than the changes which deterrents prevent or delay: a naively sweeping assumption. Naivety apart, however, it is demonstrably untrue that deterrents are never used in political innovation. New regimes often enforce change by executions or other harsh penalties. Nor will it do to shift ground slightly and say that even if deterrents are

used in this way it emphasises that they are always instruments of the faction in power. For they are also used by
terrorists, as the very name suggests.

A fourth argument is also latent rather than explicit in
the literature. It is that to be effective deterrents must
exceed the limits of what is acceptable, limits which can
be defined either in retributive or in humanitarian terms.
This argument can be considered after the two main objections have been discussed.

DO DETERRENTS DETER?

The objection which must obviously be considered first is
that deterrents do not deter. If it proved to be well-founded,
it would automatically sustain the moral objection: the
infliction of harm with the intention of deterring would
be immoral if the evidence clearly indicated that it did not
achieve this objective. (This does not mean that the moral
objection would be refuted if the evidence indicated that
deterrents are effective, or sometimes effective: it would
still be possible, as we shall see, to argue that an effective
deterrent is immoral.)

How did doubt arise about the efficacy of deterrents?
Commonsense and introspective experience seem to tell us
that of course they are effective. Almost everyone can
recall situations in which they would have infringed a law
or rule had it not been for the fear of the penalty: and
those who say they have no such recollection (as the occasional recidivist does) are regarded as abnormal, forgetful
or hypocritical.

The doubt was created by the controversy over the death
penalty. Its opponents pointed to the evidence of murder-
rates in different jurisdictions, nearly all North American,
Commonwealth or European. Though these murder-rates
varied considerably, from low to moderately high, the
existence or absence of the death penalty did not appear to

be related to these variations. Even in New Zealand, a small country where news of each murderer sentenced is publicised throughout a relatively small population, the repeated abolition and restoration of the death penalty did not seem to be related to the murder-rate.[1] From evidence such as this the conclusion was drawn that capital punishment is not a deterrent.

Those who argued in this slipshod way were reasoning as if countries had either the death penalty or no penalty. Yet as everyone knows the substitute for the death penalty is almost always a long term of imprisonment. The most that could be inferred from the evidence was that the prospect of being executed is no more effective as a deterrent than the prospect of spending many years in prison.

There is not space in a single chapter for a comprehensive review of all the published research into the efficacy of deterrents.[2] What follows is intended only as a summary of the important points that seem to be well established.

1. In spite of a good deal of quibbling over the definition of deterrence, it can be fairly simply defined as what happens when one or more people refrain[3] from some activity on one or more occasions because they fear the consequences. It is necessary to add 'on one or more occasions' because people may be deterred in some situations but not in others; 'displacement'[4] may occur, so that they are driven to seek substitutes for the activity; and this seems to be an effect that should be called deterrence, even though it falls short of what is aimed at. As for the feared consequences, three points need to be made. They can be natural (such as the consequences of

---

[1] Walker, 1968.

[2] It has been reviewed by F. E. Zimring and G. J. Hawkins (1973), J. P. Gibbs (1975) and, most thoroughly and comprehensively by D. Beyleveld (1978).

[3] Perhaps it would be convenient if the definition also included situations in which people are coerced *into* an activity through fear; but that would be too far from ordinary usage.

[4] See P. Mayhew (1976).

putting one's hand into flames) or intended by someone (for example, the damage caused by barbed wire). They may be immediate or delayed: both barbed wire and lung cancer are deterrents. They may be officially prescribed (as imprisonment is) or unofficially applied (as lynching is).

2. If people do not refrain out of fear of the consequences, they are by definition not deterred (a point to which I shall return). Sometimes, however, 'deterrence' is used to mean 'attempts to deter', of unknown efficacy, and measures are called 'deterrents' when a more precise term would be 'intended deterrents'. There are times when precision of this kind is essential; but also times when commonsense makes it unnecessary.

3. It is usual to distinguish 'general' from 'individual' (or 'special') deterrence by using the former for threats directed at people who have not experienced the unpleasant consequences and the latter for threats directed at people who have. The reason for the distinction is the assumption that people who have not experienced, say, the penalty for a crime may well be more or less responsive to the threat than those who have. Essentially, however, general and individual deterrence are attempts to do the same thing: the difference is merely that the former relies on imagination, the latter on memory.[5]

4. There are, however, more important distinctions. Clearly people may be dissuaded from some kinds of behaviour simply by being told that they are illegal or otherwise prohibited by rules whose legitimacy they acknowledge; and that is not deterrence. Nor is the attempt to educate people out of misbehaviour, unless it relies on fear of the consequences. But is it deterrence to make it more difficult to commit a crime? It depends on whether what you have in mind is the difficulty of accomplishing the crime or the difficulty of doing so undetected or unharmed. Barbed wire and fierce dogs are intended as deterrents, provided that their presence is deliberately made obvious. Burglar-proof locks are not.

[5] The difference is surely exaggerated by Zimring and Hawkins.

5. Conformity due to moral scruples is not deterrence:[6] this is true by definition. What is an empirical proposition is that where certain types of behaviour are concerned there are groups of people who because of their scruples would not indulge in it even if the risk of adverse consequences were nil. There are rich men who can afford to gamble but refrain because they believe it to be morally wrong. There are doctors who could hasten a patient's death with complete impunity but refrain because it is against their principles. There are also of course people whose principles stand up to temptation most but not all of the time. It is very hard to be sure that a given person, however strongly opposed to violence, would *in no circumstances* illegally assault another person. The most that can be said with confidence is that a lot of people conform a lot of the time for reasons other than deterrence. If we need a technical term for this phenomenon it might be 'undeterred compliance'. This would conveniently cover not only compliance due to moral scruples but also compliance due to knowledge of one's incompetence and other reasons which have nothing to do with fear.

6. More complex is the phenomenon of undeterred *non*-compliance. In some situations of extreme temptation or provocation many people commit actions which, at normal times, they know to be very likely to have dire consequences for them. We call such actions 'impulsive', and people who seem more likely than most to commit them are labelled 'impulsive': I shall use the word in this strict sense. Many acts of violence, both serious and trivial, are impulsive. It is assumed that impulsive acts cannot be influenced by deterrents; and some people so define impulsiveness that this is bound to be so. Unless, however, one rules out the possibility by definition, to what extent impulsive acts can be delayed or prevented by deterrents is a matter for research of a kind which has not been attempted.

7. To be distinguished from impulsiveness is *com*pulsiveness.

---

[6] But conformity through fear of hell is deterrence, not morality.

Some people act in a way which, even as they act, they
know to be very risky; they describe their state of mind in
terms which suggest that fear is present but is overcome by
other feelings; and in many cases their behaviour is repetitive.
Some sexual offences seem frequently to be committed in
compulsive states of mind: examples are exhibitionism and
homosexual importuning in places such as public lavatories.
The offenders' precautions show that they are aware of the
risk, but are not being deterred by it. Non-sexual examples
are found amongst gamblers, shop-lifters, rock-climbers; and
it is not too loose to describe addicts to nicotine, alcohol
or other drugs as behaving compulsively. Again, it is usually
assumed that compulsive behaviour cannot be influenced by
deterrents, although in fact it is not hard to find cases in
which the behaviour is delayed through fear of the consequences, or transferred to inconvenient places.

8. Not all undeterred non-compliance, however, is impulsive or compulsive. Some must be ascribed to simple optimism; many offenders seem unrealistically optimistic about
their chances of committing offences with impunity, in spite
of past experience. (I shall return to subjective probability
later.) Others seem to be not so much optimistic as recon-
ciled to the considerable risk. This may be so because the
penalty does not inconvenience them. An affluent motorist
may incur almost certain parking fines. A vagrant alcoholic
may have no fear of prison, which may indeed be more
comfortable and healthier than the rest of his way of life.
A recidivist thief may have lost all the prospects that make
liberty priceless. We lack precise terms for these states of
mind, which have not been studied by psychologists or
clinicians.

9. Finally there is what may be called 'defiant non-
compliance', which occurs when someone commits an
offence by way of protest in the face of an almost certain
penalty which is undoubtedly inconvenient or unpleasant.
Such offenders often have political motives; but sometimes
they simply have a less high-minded reason. Some men refuse

to pay maintenance to wives because they feel that right is on their side, whatever the law may say, and go to prison with resentful satisfaction. On the other hand, defiant non-compliance can be influenced by deterrents: the offender may choose to break one law rather than another, or in one jurisdiction rather than another, in order to lay himself open to a lesser penalty.

10. It has to be emphasised that what I have just finished describing are not people but situations and states of mind. The same person might well act impulsively, compulsively and so forth when breaking different rules or indeed when breaking the same rule in different circumstances. It is actions rather than people which are impulsive, compulsive, optimistic, defiant, despairing; and when we apply these adjectives to people, even on the, basis of their repeated behaviour, we must be careful not to delude ourselves that all their behaviour is so describable.

11. If people are deterred, then on the whole it is when they are not behaving morally, impulsively, compulsively, defiantly, despairingly or optimistically. It is hardly worth asking, no matter what sort of misbehaviour is in question, whether anyone is *ever* deterred from it: it will always be possible to find someone who can honestly say that he refrained from it because of his fear of the consequences. The sensible question is whether the number of people who calculate and can be induced to refrain when tempted to behave like that is substantial enough to make deterrence a worthwhile aim, or simply negligible.

12. What makes people refrain in such a state of mind? The nastiness of the consequences, says commonsense. Whenever the public is alarmed about some kind of crime the demand is for an increase in the severity of the penalty. Generations of penologists, however, have been stressing that the 'severity' of punishment is a less important influence than its 'certainty'. or more precisely that its *subjective probability* is more influential than its *subjective unpleasantness.* Most potential offenders are not well-informed about

the objective probability of their being convicted. Nobody is, not even statisticians: the figures are too crude. It is true that such statistical studies as we have tend to confirm that in so far as the objective probabilities of detection or conviction for serious crimes are measurable they are related in the expected way to the known rates for those crimes:[7] a fact consistent with the supposition that the objective risks affect criminal behaviour. But there are good reasons, both *a priori* (armchair) and empirical for being cautious about the universality of this relationship. Obviously, if the penalties are so mild that most people can face them without too much anxiety (as parking fines are in some jurisdictions) even a high subjective probability of incurring them will not make them an effective deterrent.

13. We know very little about the ways in which potential offenders arrive at subjective probabilities of detection, conviction and sentence. Everyday experience suggests

(a) that where ordinary risks are concerned people do not really quantify them in an arithmetical way, but simply subdivide them into rough categories, such as 'almost certain', 'high', 'low' and 'negligible';

(b) that they categorise them as a result of incidents which make a strong impression on them, for example because someone known to them is involved.

Publicised innovations such as the introduction of breathalyser tests for driving under the influence of drink achieve reductions in road accidents, especially at times in the week when people do most of their drinking, but this effect seems to wear off, no doubt because people learn that their chances of being tested are smaller than they thought at first.[8] For these reasons, attempts to achieve modest increases in detection-rates, though they may be justified on other grounds, are probably not effective deterrents. Police statistics are not widely studied, and an increase of 10 or even 20

[7] Beyleveld (1978).
[8] Ross (1970).

per cent. is probably insufficient to make potential offenders recategorise the risk.

14. Again, it is not always safe to assume that what appears to us more severe seems so to potential offenders. Willcock[9] found that many males in their late teens feared probation more than fines (perhaps because they could rely on their parents to contribute to fines, and saw probation as a real inconvenience). On the whole, however, it seems safer to assume that most potential offenders fear a custodial sentence more than a non-custodial one, and a long custodial sentence more than a short one; and there is a little empirical evidence to support this.[10] On the other hand, the evidence — as we have seen — does not support the armchair assumption that many reflective murderers fear death more than 'life'. At the other end of the scale it is frequently said that where stigmatising offences are concerned the mere prospect of conviction is the deterrent rather than the likely penalty: Willcock's survey seemed to confirm this so far as many teenage males were concerned, but it was not true of all his sample, and would probably prove untrue when severe penalties were very likely.

15. How much then do we know about situations in which people do refrain from actions through fear of penalties or other consequences? Obviously we can learn very little about them by studying situations in which people have committed such actions. It might be more profitable to ask known recidivists to recall occasions on which they had *refrained* from committing offences of a kind about which they clearly had no moral scruples; but this has seldom been tried,[11] and

[9] Willcock (1963).
[10] Beyleveld (1978).
[11] Repetto (1974) interviewed 97 convicted burglars on these lines, with instructive results. W. Knapp and I arranged interviews with 18 acquisitive recidivist prisoners, who were asked to describe incidents in which they had seriously contemplated theft, robbery etc. but had refrained. About half could not recall any such occasion; but the rest could. In some cases they had decided that they lacked the expertise:

only in a very limited way. The difficulties are obvious.

16. There are a number of studies in which subjects have been asked such questions as

(a) whether, or how often, they have done X (*e.g.,* smoked cannabis);

(b) what their estimate is of the risk of detection;

(c) what the likely penalty is.

In this way, Waldo and Chiricos[12] found that Florida State University undergraduates who said they had never used cannabis were more likely than those who said they had

(i) to estimate the risk of detection as high; and

(ii) to over-estimate the likely penalty.

Unfortunately this does not indicate which was cause and which was effect: non-users may have been deterred by high estimates of risks and penalties, or their estimates may simply have been less realistic because they were non-users. The problem is one which this method finds it difficult to overcome.

17. Two large groups of studies are based on official statistics of recorded crimes. One group compares *per capita* rates of such crimes in different jurisdictions with different detection-rates and different maximum penalties for the crime in question. Some problems of this method are

(i) to allow for the effects of other variables, such as the proportions of under-privileged groups (*e.g.,* non-whites) which tend to be over-represented in the statistics for the crime in question;

(ii) to take into account the unknown percentages of un-reported crimes, which obviously make detection-rates inaccurate;

(iii) to take into account the difference between the

one man for instance had planned to mug a cashier on his way from a shop to a bank, but at the last minute realised that he had no idea how to attack him effectively. Others had simply come to the conclusion that the odds were against them, for instance because they saw someone who recognised them just as they were about to commit the crime.

[12] Waldo and Chiricos (1972).

maximum permitted sentence and the likely actual sentence. This is especially difficult where even the length of the prison sentence actually imposed by the court is shortened by variable amounts (as happens when parole operates).

18. The other body of studies which rely on similar data concentrates on their fluctuations over time in the same jurisdiction. This reduces the effect of variables such as under-reporting, under-privileged groups, or differences between maximum and actual penalties, although if the time-series is a long one these may undergo major changes, either gradually or as a result of legislation or other developments.

Studies of these kinds are not very satisfactory. It is true that the majority find the inverse correlations between rates of recorded crime and the probability[13] of penalties which one would expect if deterrence were taking place. In the first place, however, these correlations are not strong; but unfortunately it is not possible to tell whether this is because

(i) the majority of criminals are insensitive to (or too knowledgeable about) risks and severity;

or (ii) the variations in risks and severity are not marked enough to have a strong effect;

or (iii) recorded crimes are a rather inaccurate index of the crimes which are actually being committed, due to variations in reporting by the public and recording by police.

Moreover, it has recently been suggested that here again the research workers have assumed too hastily that the cause-effect relationship must be one in which the recorded crime-rates represent the effect, whereas the reverse may be nearer the truth. Pontell[14] has suggested what he calls a 'system-capacity model' in which it is high crime-rates that cause lower probabilities of detection, and lower probabilities of penalties such as imprisonment, by *overburdening the*

[13] And in some cases also the severity.
[14] Pontell (1978). See also, however, the criticisms of his article in the same issue.

capacity of the law enforcement system. He claims that the data support this model more strongly than the deterrence model.

More conclusive are time-series in which one or other of the crucial variables is deliberately altered to such an extent, and with such publicity, that it can be safely presumed that many potential offenders' estimates of it must have been altered. Extreme examples are provided by police strikes, which drastically but temporarily reduce the risk of apprehension for robbers and thieves: sure enough, up go the rates of such crimes[15] during the strikes. An example of a sudden *increase* in the subjective probability of detection was the already mentioned introduction of the breathalyser test in Britain in October, 1967 (accompanied by a mandatory disqualification from driving): this was followed by a marked reduction in serious road accidents, especially on week-end nights, when most alcohol is drunk; but the reduction was not maintained, at least at the same level.[16]

19. Such time-series have been called 'quasi-experiments', because − as in an experiment − one or more of the important variables has been subjected to a marked change, although not for experimental reasons. Genuine experiments in deterrence have also been carried out. They have been of two kinds. In 'laboratory' experiments, subjects − usually children or students − have been given tasks involving temptations to infringe prohibitions (for example, to cheat in order to get a prize), but the risks of detection have been varied. The advantage of such experiments is the greater control which the experimenter has over the variables which he wants to keep constant. Their weakness is the artificiality of the experimental situations (for instance the necessity for instructing subjects in a way that is alien to everyday life), and the subjects' knowledge that they are the objects of special attention of some sort. Thus, though the experimental findings

[15] But not of crimes such as embezzlement, which are detected not by police but by auditors, and reported when the police return to work.
[16] Ross (1970).

are usually consistent with the hypothesis that deterrence is at work, they are not strong confirmation of the operation of deterrence in real life.

20. 'Real life' experiments, in which the important variables have been deliberately manipulated in a planned way, and the measurement of effects has been organised before hand, are difficult to arrange, and only a few worthwhile examples have been reported.[17] Three involved alterations in the concentration of police patrols, and in two out of the three these alterations were accompanied by changes in recorded crime which were consistent with deterrence. (In the third case the absence of the expected changes could be explained in a special way.) In one other experiment − in which the police of three Finnish towns dealt more leniently than usual with drunks − the findings seem to indicate that the drunks had not noticed the difference in police behaviour: a good illustration of the danger of assuming that changes in objective risks will affect subjective probabilities.

In the other four experiments the results were clearly consistent with the supposition that deterrence was at work. The best of them was achieved by Schwartz and Orleans[18] with the help of the United States Internal Revenue Service. Nearly 400 tax-payers were divided into four matched groups. Members of the 'sanction' group were interviewed, and asked questions designed to remind them indirectly of the penalties which they might suffer if they tried to evade taxes. Members of the 'conscience' group were interviewed with questions designed to arouse their civic sense and feelings of duty. The third, or 'placebo' group were asked only neutral questions, which avoided both sorts of stimulus. The fourth group were not interviewed at all, in order to test the possibility that even a 'placebo' interview produced some effect (which on the whole it did not seem to do). The interviews took place in the month before the taxpayers were

[17] At least in English: see Beyleveld (1978)
[18] Schwartz and Orleans (1967).

due to file their returns for 1962. Without disclosing information about individuals, the Internal Revenue Service compared the returns of the four groups for the year before the experiment and the year 1962. The reported gross incomes of both the 'sanction' and the 'conscience' groups showed an increase, compared with small decreases in the 'placebo' and uninterviewed groups. In other words, the attempts to stimulate fear of penalties and civic conscience both seemed to have had effect.[19]

An equally thorough experiment was carried out by Buikhuisen[20] in Groningen, in the Netherlands. He persuaded the police to launch a campaign against illegally worn tyres, and the newspapers to publicise the results of the police checks. A similar town, Leeuwarden, was chosen as a control, and it was established before the experiment that the rates at which motorists spontaneously renewed worn tyres were very similar in both towns. The result of the police campaign was a far higher rate of renewal in Groningen than in Leeuwarden (where there was no campaign and no publicity for the Groningen campaign). Samples of compliers and non-compliers were interviewed; and it was found that significantly more of the non-compliers

   (i) did not know of the campaign;
   (ii) said they would go on using worn tyres even in the event of a future campaign;
   (iii) were younger;
   (iv) were less well educated;
   (v) drove old, second-hand cars which were badly maintained in other important respects.

This seems to confirm the existence of a group of undeterrible non-compliers (see point 6 above). The only important

---

[19] They drew a slightly bolder conclusion: that appeals to conscience were more effective than threat of sanctions; but this inference assumes that the appeal and the threat were of equal potency, whereas it is conceivable that unintentionally they had made their 'conscience' interview a more powerful stimulus.

[20] Buikhuisen (1974).

defect in the experiment is that it did not exclude the possibility that a substantial number of instances of compliance took place not because the compliers were deterred but because they were *reminded* of the desirability of renewing worn tyres; and the interviewers do not seem to have discussed this possibility with them.

THE BEST EVIDENCE

In short, when real-life experiments have created situations in which common sense would expect that compliance with a rule would increase in frequency as a result of a recent increase in some people's estimate of the probability of being detected in and penalised for non-compliance, the findings have been consistent with this expectation. The same is broadly true of quasi-experiments.

This sounds a little weak. It seems suspicious that social scientists cannot come up with a positive proof of the operation of deterrence in specified situations. In their defence it can be argued that in the nature of things this would be very difficult. In the natural sciences, as Popper has pointed out, the experimental method tests hypotheses by trying to disprove them. Failure to disprove increases confidence in the hypothesis: success in disproving leads to a change of hypothesis and further tests. Experiments have not disproved the hypothesised operation of deterrence, as defined in the previous paragraph, and should therefore increase our confidence in it.

This may not be the whole story, however, where social science is concerned. The natural sciences deal with inanimate or inarticulate things, whereas human beings consciously experience motivation, and can be asked about their reasons for their acts or omissions, as they are in everyday life. It is true that the answers are not always trustworthy: people are not always able or willing to be honest about their motivation. But if both subjects' behaviour and the reasons they give for it point in the same direction, a real-life experiment could provide something very close to confirmation of the operation of deterrence. In Buikhuisen's experiment, to take the most suitable example, samples of his subjects were interviewed. If those who had renewed their worn tyres had been asked why they had done so, the number who mentioned fear of police action would have been very relevant. Substantial or negligible numbers would have indicated the extent to which the increased compliance in Groningen was due to deterrence.

To sum up, it is only from real-life experiments (*i.e.*, not quasi- or laboratory experiments, and not statistical comparisons of jurisdictions or studies of time-series) that we can expect strong indications of the extent to which deterrence operates and the variables which affect it. The few fairly sound experiments so far reported are consistent with the commonsense expectation that compliance will increase in frequency with a recent increase in some people's estimate of the probability of being detected and penalised if they do not comply. But we need experiments in which subjects are asked the right questions, and not merely manipulated as if they were inanimate objects.

This disposes, at least for the time being, of the argument that deterrents are immoral because they involve the deliberate infliction of suffering for a purpose which they cannot achieve. At most the evidence suggests that extreme penalties, such as death, are no more effective than slightly less extreme ones, such as long incarceration. Otherwise the evidence is consistent, as has been said, with a belief in the limited operation of deterrence.

DETERRENCE AS HUMAN SACRIFICE

This does not, however, answer the moralist who concedes that deterrence benefits those who would otherwise be victims of crime, but points out that it does not benefit the criminals who suffer the deterrent penalties.[21] He might argue that we no longer regard it as right to compel people to sacrifice themselves unwillingly for the benefit of the societies to which they belong. Sacrifices must be voluntary. Vaccination and inoculation are no longer compulsory for Britons in spite of the death and impairment which they would save. Conscientious objectors to service in the armed forces are no longer conscripted even in wars.

This is probably an oversimplification. Vaccination and inoculation are no longer compulsory, but quarantine can be; and typhoid carriers in catering jobs can be compelled to find other occupations. Conscientious objectors may be excused from killing but required to perform other tasks which help an embattled society, such as ambulance work. It is expediency rather than morality which has prompted these concessions. Conscientious objectors are a nuisance in the armed services. Compulsory vaccination was unpopular, troublesome and eventually unnecessary. We do not think it immoral to require many minor and some not so minor acts of self-sacrifice: examples are jury service, currency restrictions, food rationing, or the compulsory purchase of homes as part of replanning operations.

Is there something special about the involuntary sacrifices involved in deterrents which makes them morally objectionable? Kant is often quoted in support of the view that there is:

'... Punishment can never be administered merely as a means for promoting another Good, either with regard to the Criminal himself or to Civil Society, but must in all cases be imposed only because the individual on whom it is inflicted has committed a Crime. For one man ought never to be dealt with merely as a means subservient to the purpose of

---

[21] Except to the extent that some of them are saved from being the victims of others' crimes.

another, not be mixed up with the subjects of Real Right [*i.e.,* goods or property]. Against such treatment his Inborn Personality has a Right to protect him, even although he may be condemned to lose his Civil Personality. He must first be found guilty and punishable, before there can be any thought of drawing from his punishment any benefit for himself or his fellow citizens.'[2 2]

It should be noticed, however, that what Kant is condemning is the use of punishment *merely* as a means of promoting, say, the good of society. He seems to concede that once a person has been found guilty and punishable it is not reprehensible to think of 'drawing from his punishment ... benefit for himself or his fellow citizens'. As Hart says '... Kant never made the mistake of saying that we must never treat men as means. He insisted that we should never treat them *only* as means, "but in every case as ends also"'.[2 3]

PERSONS AS ENDS

If so, deterrents are morally objectionable *only if their use is incompatible with treating men as ends*. This raises the question 'What did Kant mean by treating a person as an end?'; or rather, since Kant is dead but his viewpoint survives, however imprecisely, 'What sensible meaning can now be attached to these words?' For Kant almost certainly meant 'punishing them retributively as morally responsible agents'.[2 4] Since it would be a pity to beg the whole question by assuming the primacy of the retributive justification of punishment, let us consider non-Kantian versions:

(i) that penal systems should deal with people as if they

[2 2] *Rechtslehre* (1797).
[2 3] (1968).
[2 4] See T. Honderich's discussion of what he meant (1976).

were rational actors cognisant of (if not necessarily sub-
scribing to) the laws of the society in which they live.
But this version would not merely be compatible with the
use of penalties as deterrents; it would tend to support it. If
people act rationally, and know the laws and the penalties
for breaking them, it is arguable that we acknowledge and
honour this by deterrents, and certainly more so than by
attempts at reform: that we are in effect treating offenders
as having voluntarily chosen to risk penalties as the price of
disobedience.

Obviously it is fictional to proceed as if all law-breakers
voluntarily choose this risk. The impulsive and compulsive
do not; nor do those who fail to realise that they are breaking
the law. Officially the law presumes that people know what
is prohibited and intend the natural consequences of their
acts; but sentencers are usually more realistic, and mitigate
penalties in cases of pardonable ignorance of the law or
thoughtless actions. This is not inconsistent with a policy
of penalising intentional law-breakers in deterrent ways;
and it does not mean that interpretation (i) rules this out:
merely that to impose deterrents on *all* law-breakers would
be going too far.

The second non-Kantian interpretation of 'treating a
person as an end' is:

(ii) that penal measures should have regard to the welfare
of the people subjected to them.

This could either have a strong or a weak meaning. In its
strong form it would in effect be saying that no penalty
should operate to the detriment of the offender himself.
Only penalties which conferred benefits on him, whether
spiritual or material, should be used. This would allow
reformative measures but not the deliberate infliction of
loss or hardship in order to deter others. If it were intended
to deter the offender himself from further law-breaking it
would have to be shown to be likely that the deterrent
penalty was less injurious than the non-penal consequences
of future law breaking to the offender. This would limit

individual deterrents to cases in which the penalised behaviour was likely to damage the offender's health, finances
or social relations.[25]

RETRIBUTIVE OR HUMANITARIAN LIMITS

Even if the strong version seems to go too far, interpretation
(ii) does seem to express a feeling which a lot of people have
about deterrents, a feeling that in order to be effective they
must often exceed the limits of what is morally acceptable.
I referred to this earlier as the fourth moral argument against
deterrence, and it seems to be concerned, as interpretation
(ii) is, with the offender's own welfare. It implies that if the
limits of what is acceptable by way of imposed loss, suffering
or hardship could be defined, some intended deterrents
might be found to fall within them, some beyond them.

But how and where are the limits set? If by retributive
considerations, proportionality[26] will merely dictate that
the deterrent penalty for illegal parking should be less severe
than that for reckless driving, and so on. In extreme cases it
will also dictate that the harm done to the offender should
not exceed the harm which he intended or consciously risked.

More often, the limits which are envisaged seem to be
humanitarian rather than retributive. Do they involve any
principles that can be put into general terms? If we list the
kinds or aspects of deterrent penalties to which humane
objections are most often raised, they seem to be

a. death, mutilation and other corporal punishments;
b. permanently stigmatising penalties;
c. penalties which impose hardship on innocent depen-
    dants or associates as well as on the defender.

Deterrents such as fines, which have no permanent or

---

[25] *e.g.*, misuse of alcohol or drugs. But individual deterrents are
not very effective in such cases.
[26] See Sir Rupert Cross (1975, 117–118).

stigmatising effects, do not seem to arouse moral objections. It seems possible to define the target of humanitarian objections as harm which is bodily, life-long or spread to non-offenders.

This would rule out capital punishment, flogging, the amputation of hands, the deliberate penalising of, say, offenders' families, and detention for periods or under conditions which are likely to have permanent ill-effects. It would not rule out fines fixed with due regard to offenders' situations, short periods of detention in decent conditions, compulsory service to the community, disqualification from driving[27] or other common deterrents.

The weak form of interpretation (ii) would also involve a duty to do what is possible to ensure that the harm done by deterrents is limited, as far as is practicable, to the offender himself and to a tolerable period.[28]

SUMMARY

I have argued
  a. that the prejudice against deterrents is due to their historical association with penalties which exceed what are now regarded as humanitarian limits;
  b. that their alleged association with the preservation of the political *status quo* is nonsense;
  c. that the objection to them which is based on the assumption that they are ineffective is too sweeping;
  d. that the moral objection that deterrents compulsorily sacrifice offenders' welfare to the welfare of others ignores the extent to which societies demand compulsory sacrifices from non-offenders;

[27] It may be pointed out that disqualification from driving was intended by the legislature as a means of protection, not as a deterrent. That does not mean, however, that it does not operate as a deterrent.
[28] This has implications for the control of stigma: that is discussed in Chapter 7.

e. that the Kantian objection can be sustained only by the pure retributavist who believes that the only justifying aim of penalties can be to impose appropriate punishment,

f. that the utilitarian version of the Kantian objection can take the form of an ˙insistence that offenders be dealt with as rational actors cognisant of the law, but that this actually supports the use of deterrents in most cases;

g. that it rules out deterrents only if it takes the extreme form of an insistence that no penalty should operate to the detriment of the offender himself;

h. that if it takes the weaker (but more reasonable) form of an insistence that penalties should not impose harm which is bodily, life-long or spread to non-offenders it does not rule out several deterrents commonly in use.

APPENDIX

An aspect of deterrence which has not been discussed, in order to avoid complicating consideration of the really important problems, is the question whether deterring potential *victims* from rendering themselves vulnerable to offences is open to objections which are not relevant where the deterrence of potential offenders is the problem. West Germany allows motorists to be penalised for leaving their cars unlocked and thus facilitating thefts. It is arguable that this is an economical way of combating such thefts. But does it not come close to the use of deterrents against the innocent? The motorist could argue that if he cares to risk the theft of his car or its contents that is his business. This is not entirely so, especially if he troubles the police about the theft, or makes claims on his insurance company. It is also possible that by making theft easy he is encouraging car thieves to commit thefts which will harm other motorists.

These counter-arguments may seem slightly thin. But consider the somewhat different case of the legitimate owner of firearms or explosives who can be penalised for not taking steps to prevent them from being stolen. If stolen they are likely to be used in illegitimate and dangerous ways. Most people would consider that this justifies penalties for insecure keeping of firearms or explosives. But it involves deterring people who have no criminal intentions from providing opportunities for those who have. Is it justifiable only by an appeal to expediency, or can some more high-minded principle be invoked?

5 Protecting

If — as so often happens — someone opens his discussion of a concept by reciting a dictionary's definition, this suggests to me that he himself is unsure what he is talking about. In any case, if the concept is sufficiently controversial to merit discussion, the dictionary is probably misleading. Dictionaries are after all compiled by people in back rooms, consulting publications rather than listening to contemporary conversations. Even when they look at the printed word they seldom think of legal usage.

In the case of 'dangerousness' this is especially striking. One author, for example, begins an otherwise excellent article with the Oxford Dictionary's definition of 'danger' as 'power of a lord or master (dominium)': a usage which is so archaic — to use that Dictionary's own term — that it has ceased to have any relevance to the modern meaning. Equally out of date and irrelevant are such meanings as '1. Liability (to loss)... 2. Difficulty...chariness, coyness...'

Even '3. Mischief or harm' is out of date. In modern usage, a danger is not an actual mischief or harm, but one which is possible or likely. A dangerous situation, action or activity is one which makes some kind of harm more likely than usual.

Nor are we thinking of any kind of harm when we use the word 'danger'. We usually have in mind serious and not trivial harm. Betting a small sum of money on an 'outsider' is merely 'risky': it is risking all or most of one's capital that that would be 'dangerous'. Climbing over a barbed wire fence is not dangerous: driving across a railway line in front of an approaching train is.

The likelihood of harm, however, must be more than negligible. Investing all one's money in Government loan stock is not dangerous: nor is driving across a railway line when the signal indicates that this is safe. Our whole lives are surrounded by innumerable but negligible possibilities of dreadful harm; but we do not regard ourselves as living dangerously. A dangerous situation, action or activity is one which raises the probability of serious harm above a certain level.

To define that level is not easy, but perhaps not impossible. It is the level which causes a person who is not neurotically or superstitiously anxious to become so apprehensive that he explores the possibility of avoiding the situation, action or activity. Obviously this level varies with the nature of the apprehended harm. The threshold is lower for rabies than for jaundice: higher for a broken neck than a broken leg.

It is tempting to say, pseudo-scientifically, that *danger = seriousness X probability of harm*. This ignores one fact however: that if either seriousness or probability is below a certain level we do not think of the situation as dangerous. It also assumes that the relationship is multiplicative, whereas we do not know this. Research might conceivably show that a more complex mathematical expression would fit our way of thinking about danger: but it would merely lend precision to what is already sufficiently obvious.

DANGEROUSNESS AND PENOLOGY

In penology the concept of dangerousness presents legislators with two problems. One is the selection of activities for inclusion in the criminal law; the other is the selection of people for special measures of control. The state of play, however, is quite different in each case. It is universally accepted that certain activities should be made criminal because of the grave harms which they may cause. Examples are the importation without quarantine of animals which may be carrying rabies or other fatal diseases; or the manufacture of toxic substances without precautions against the exposure of the public to them. Such disagreement as exists is concerned mainly with the list of such activities and the machinery of control. This is not to overlook the question of the extent to which decisions may be biassed by commercial, political or ideological interests. The point for the moment, however, is that nobody denies the necessity for legislative control of a large number of activities because of their 'dangerousness'.

DANGEROUS PEOPLE

On the other hand, a lot of people question the ethics of labelling a specified individual as dangerous in order to justify special measures of control. Their arguments vary. Some hold that labelling a man as dangerous can make him more so, or even make a dangerous man out of a non-dangerous one: see for example Sarbin, 1967. The way in which he is treated by police and prison staff can make him respond aggressively to any attempts to control him, or indeed to other forms of frustration when he is at liberty again. This is not, however, an argument against labelling anyone as dangerous, but against careless labelling and certain techniques of inmate-management.

More to the point is the argument that dangerousness should never be ascribed to people, only to situations, actions or activities. It is this argument that has to be taken seriously, if only because it is taken seriously.

It is a very sweeping argument, and contrary to normal usage. We not only call things like unexploded bombs or rickety bridges 'dangerous': we apply the term to some animals and some people. If pressed we can usually say what the danger is: that a horse may kick or bolt, for example, or that a man may do violence or commit a very harmful indiscretion.

What is said to be wrong with this usage is that it 'objecti-fies' the danger, by talking as if it were a characteristic of the person, instead of something that he might do in certain circumstances. If so, there must be the same objection to calling people 'loyal', 'truthful', 'irritable' or 'deceitful'. We do not mean that they are always behaving loyally, truth-fully, irritably or deceitfully: only that this is how they usually behave in circumstances which test those qualities.

Nor do we mean, as objectors sometimes assume, that a man who is labelled as dangerously violent will inevitably injure someone who annoys or frustrates him. Not only do we make allowances for circumstances — such as the presence or absence of a policeman — but we also recognise the fact that a man's self-control varies, so that one day he will react violently to an insult which on another day he might swallow. All that we mean is that he is more likely than most people we know — or know of — to react violently.

Sometimes of course — but fortunately not often — we are talking about people who do not merely do harm as a reaction to a situation, but about people who seek out oppor-tunities for harm. Some men go out looking for a fight; a few sexual offenders actively seek out victims. There are opportunity-takers and opportunity-makers as well as reactors.

THE ETHICAL ISSUE

If on the other hand the real objection is not to linguistic usage but to policies based on labelling people as dangerous, this deserves a much more serious discussion. What gives rise to understandable misgivings in penology and psychiatry is the fact — and it *is* a fact — that in the name of public pro-tection psychiatrists, sentencers, parole authorities, are detaining people against their will *for longer periods than they can justify on other grounds.* Let us accept, if only for the sake of argument, that detention for some length of time can be justified as what the offender deserves, or as a declaration of society's disapproval, or as a deterrent, or as the only way of ensuring treatment for a disorder (according to the circumstances, one's moral philosophy, or one's therapeutic optimism). The fuss is about prolongation of the detention beyond the time regarded as required to expiate the crime, declare the disapproval, provide a deterrent, or carry out the treatment.

This issue is recognized rather than faced in the publication of the Canadian Law Reform Commission called *Our Criminal Law.* In its excellent concluding section it says:

> 'Criminal law operates at three different stages. At the law-making stage it denounces and prohibits certain actions. At the trial stage it condemns in solemn ritual those who commit them. And at the punishment stage it penalizes the offenders. This, not mere deterrence and rehabilitation, is what we get from criminal law ...'

Throughout the report it is assumed that the aims of sentencing are deterrence, denunciation and rehabilitation. When we come to imprisonment, however, the notion of public protection is introduced: imprisonment, we are told, must be used only

> '... where necessary — for offenders too dangerous to leave at large, too wilful to submit to other sanctions, or too wrongful to be adequately condemned by non-custodial sentences.'

In short, public protection as a justifiable aim is ignored, and its problems left undiscussed, yet it is taken for granted as a justification for imprisonment.

Of course, in societies which regard very long prison sentences as justified on other ground, the problem need not be faced. By the time the offender is released, one or more things will have happened. He will be a lot older; and with increasing age everyone's capacity for doing physical harm is increasingly restricted. He will be to some extent institutionalised, which means in this context more compliant with rules, showing less initiative, and less in touch with current facilities — for example, for obtaining firearms illegally. If his violence, or sexual desire, was directed at specific people, such as his wife or daughters, they will probably be beyond his reach by then. If he was simply regarded as a danger to women, or children, or people in general, the public will by the time of his release be frightened of someone else, although it must be granted that alarm is sometimes revived by newspapers whose filing systems are superior to their motives.

What has made the concept of dangerousness a really live issue is the shortening of the periods of detention which legislators, sentencers and psychiatrists regard as justified on other grounds. Whether the retributive approach to sentencing is becoming less prevalent or not, those who still adhere to it seem to be lowering their tariffs. Those who maintain that the fundamental justification for imprisonment is that it declares society's moral values also seem to be using a reduced price list. As for deterrence, we have learned to question the assumption that the difference between a three-year and a ten-year sentence is crucial; and when one reflects that potential offenders are knowledgeable, not to say optimistic, about remission and parole, this is not surprising. Finally, therapeutic claims are now more modest. More and more psychiatrists are prepared to admit that if they cannot produce marked improvements within the first six months[1] of treatment, they will not do so thereafter, however long they try. As for non-psychiatric 'treatment', penologists are increasingly sceptical about its efficacy in dealing with most

[1] '...any significant improvement is likely to take place in the first 6 months' says the Department of Health and Social Security in *A Review of the Mental Health Act, 1959*.

kinds of law-breaking. All of which means that if you want to
detain someone for, say, ten years most of that period now
has to be justified by the claim that you are protecting others
by doing so.

But one may be forgiven for asking what is wrong with
that claim. Why shouldn't the protection of the public be
regarded as a justification which is quite as sound as retribution, deterrence, or the need for treatment? There is an
answer which is based, fundamentally, on the argument that
you may have a right to detain someone for something which
he *has* done, or at least attempted or risked by his recklessness or negligence, but not for something which he *has not*
done but might do. As a Swedish judge once put it to me in
conversation, 'you are punishing him for a crime which he
hasn't committed'. In this form the argument is clearly retributive, and, what is more, retributive in the traditional
Kantian way. Modern retributivism insists that sentences
must be restricted to people who break the law with *mens rea*,
but does not insist that the nature or length of the sentence
must be commensurate with their wickedness. It allows that
once you have given the state the right to sentence you, that
sentence may be shaped by other aims, such as deterrence
or reform; and if by such aims, why not by the aim of protecting others? It is only the traditional retributivist who
insists that the form or length of the sentence must be
limited by proportionality to one's wickedness.

The Swedish judge's point of view however cannot be
dismissed simply by labelling it traditional. What has to be
pointed out is that it seeks to impose restrictions on the law-
enforcement system which we do not impose on other social
institutions. The most obvious example is the compulsory
commitment of certain mentally disordered people when this
is done to protect others. Sometimes they are so disordered
that even the most retributive moralist would concede that
they are guiltless. But since the detention of the mentally
disordered is one of the subjects of this controversy I had
better add examples which are not. One is the disqualifica-

tion of epileptics from driving. Another is the restrictions which we place on people who are known or suspected to carry diseases with a high mortality rate, such as smallpox, typhoid, lassa fever, or Marburg virus. The traditional retributivist, who asserts that the law enforcement system ought not to take account of the harm which people might do, must either explain why it should be subject to a restrictive principle which we do not apply outside the system, or else argue that we should apply the same principle outside it.

That may dispose of the retributivist who calls protective measures punishment for uncommitted crimes; but that is not the only objection to protection as a justification. Another extreme one is that we ought never to classify anyone as dangerous, and, therefore, ought never to subject anyone to compulsory measures aimed solely at the safety of others. In its pure form, as we have seen, this argument is sometimes expressed by saying that there are no dangerous people, only dangerous actions. If all that is meant by this is that nobody is ever *certain* to do harm to others in the future, it is acceptable. Something may always intervene, whether it is a change of circumstances or a change of heart. But if it means that we can never say of anyone 'unless something very unlikely happens to prevent him, that man is going to kill or seriously injure somebody within the next year or two', then it goes too far.

After all, we make very confident predictions about other sorts of behaviour. We lend money to people – some people anyway – because we know that unless they drop dead, or are stricken with amnesia, they will pay us back. We assume that people will do what they say they will do, whether they are debtors or terrorists.

It is proper of course to draw a distinction between someone who says 'I'll pay you back' or 'I'm going to fight for the liberation of my country with bombs and bullets', and on the other hand the sort of prisoner, or patient, who says, 'I don't want to commit another assault (or rape or whatever act brought him inside), but I know that in certain circumstances I won't be able to help myself'. He differs in two ways from the man who declares his intention to do something nasty. First, on the assumption that he is telling the truth about his intentions, he is morally less responsible if he does do it. Second, he is usually less likely to do it, because, whereas, the intentional terrorist will probably try to *make* opportunities for what he is liable to do, the other man is more likely to *avoid* opportunities if he foresees them in time. There are exceptions: some sexual offenders' behaviour is extremely compulsive: but fortunately the compulsive behaviour usually takes relatively harmless forms, such as exhibitionism.

Both these groups, however (*i.e.,* those who declare intentions and those who confess their inability to resist impulses or compulsions) must be distinguished from the sort of person who truthfully denies that he is conscious of a desire to repeat what he has done. He may believe that his violence was the natural, even inevitable, outcome of an unusual situation in which he found himself; and it may indeed be the case that this is the only sort of situation in which he has behaved violently. It is this type of case which provides the anti-protectionists with their strongest talking-point. For not only is intentional personal violence by an adult a comparatively rare event (at least in a society which is not at war); it is even rarer for an adult who has been officially identified with such violence to be associated with violence on a later occasion. The same seems to be true of sexual offences which involve the serious molestation of unwilling victims. Reconvictions for violent or serious[2] sexual offences are much rarer than reconvictions for dishonesty or traffic offences: and it is most unlikely that this can be explained to any important extent by differences in reporting-rates.

More precisely, not only is there no definable category of violent or sexual offender of whom it can be predicted with

_____

[2] I say 'serious' because this may not be true of male exhibitionism or female soliciting.

certainty that he will do similar harm in the future: there is only one definable category at present of whom this can be predicted with even a high probability: the defender who declares his intention of doing it again. This is in contrast to dishonest offenders: it is not difficult to define groups of men of whom at least two-thirds will be reconvicted of dishonesty within a few years. All one has to do is to define them as males with four or five previous convictions for dishonesty. If you predict of the members of such a group that they will behave dishonestly again, you will be right a good deal more often than wrong. But with violence the reverse is the case: nobody has so far reliably defined in this way a group of violent males with a probability of further violence approaching even 50 percent.[3] In other words, we have not yet succeeded in providing criteria which would ensure that a prediction of future violence would be right more often than it would be wrong. With present criteria, it would more often be wrong.

This being so, the anti-protectionists argue, a period of custody, or an extension of custody, which is imposed solely in order to protect others against violence will be *unnecessarily* imposed in the majority of cases. Put more strongly, it will mean detaining two or three (or even more) individuals in order to prevent only one of them from committing further violence.[4]

This sounds like irresistible arithmetic. But it is arithmetic with limitations. In the first place, it must be pointed out that the attempts to find criteria that would define high-risk groups have not been very thorough. They have been improvised pieces of research based on data which happened to be available. In fairness, it must be said that it is very difficult

[3] David Steer and I once identified a sample of violent Scots with a 55 percent probability of reconviction for violence; but the numbers were small and the study has not been replicated.

[4] For a strongly argued example of the anti-protectionist case see Professor A. E. Bottoms' Inaugural Lecture 'Reflections on the Renaissance of Dangerousness'.

indeed to design a piece of research which would meet the required standards of thoroughness. The difficulties include the relative infrequency of repeated violence; the very natural unwillingness of penal systems or hospitals to release violent inmates in an experimental way; the lack of reliable information about the situations in which the violence occurred; the still greater lack of information about the situations in which the violence occurred; the still greater lack of information about violence which did not lead to prosecution or admission to hospital. Nevertheless, the likelihood is that a thorough, large-scale piece of research, designed specifically for this purpose, would succeed in producing criteria that would enable us to define groups with a future violence rate substantially over 50 percent, so that we could at least be right more often than we would be wrong. The groups would be numerically small; and would still not include the majority of violent individuals. But it would be a very desirable advance.

The second answer to the anti-protectionist's arithmetic is more fundamental. Let us accept that in our present state of partial ignorance any labelling of the individual as a future perpetrator of violence is going to be mistaken in the ma-jority of cases. Does it follow that it is wrong to apply this label? Only if we swallow two assumptions. One is that it is *morally wrong* to make mistakes of this kind. Everyone would agree that it is *regrettable*; but if the decision is taken with good intentions, and one has done one's best, with the available information, to minimise the percentage of mistaken detentions, is it *morally wrong*? Only if we swallow the second assumption — namely the anti-protectionist's insistence that our over-riding objective must be to minimise the total number of mistaken decisions, treating a mistaken decision to detain as exactly equal to a mistaken decision to release. The anti-protectionist is using two neat rhetorical tricks at once. By referring to mistaken detentions and mistaken releases simply as 'mistakes', he is implying that they all count the same; and by glossing over the difference between 'regrettable' and 'morally wrong', he is implying that it is our moral duty to go for the smallest number of mistakes irrespective of their nature.

To put this point in concrete terms, suppose that you have in custody three men who have done serious violence to more or less innocent victims. Suppose too that the best actuarial information you can get tells you that one of them – but not *which* one – will do more violence if released. The anti-protectionist is saying that it is your moral duty to release all three instead of continuing to detain all three because release will involve only one mistaken decision instead of two mistaken decisions. Yet the one mistaken release would mean injury or death to someone, while the two mistaken detentions would mean something quite different: the continued deprivation of freedom for three men of whom an unidentifiable two would not do anybody injury if released.[5] It is natural, perhaps even morally right, to look for rules on which to base such difficult decisions; but arithmetic will not make them for us. The most it can do is to give us some idea of the magnitude of the risks involved in each of the choices we are faced with. I shall suggest in a minute what sorts of rules can help us further towards rational decisions, but there are two more anti-arithmetical points to be made.

For another rhetorical technique is to terrify us with large numbers. Dr Megargee, in an otherwise excellent article,[6] asks us to consider what would happen if tests devised by Dr Kozol, which yield only about 50 percent of false positives, were applied to a random sample of 100,000

---

[5] And those who support retribution in its distributive form, advocated by Hart, would add 'three men who after all by a deliberate act of violence have given us the right to detain them'.

[6] See his article, 'The Prediction of Dangerous Behaviour', *Criminal Justice and Behaviour* (1976) *3*: 3. He is referring to H. Kozol *et al.*, 'The Diagnosis and Treatment of Dangerousness', *Crime and Delinquency* (1972) *18*: 371, as updated in a personal communication from Dr Kozol to Dr Megargee.

citizens. According to Megargee's arithmetic, this would wrongly identify nearly 50,000 people as future perpetrators of violence. This certainly means that, quite apart from morality, the application of such a test to the general population is out of the question on political and economic grounds. But is anyone seriously proposing an exercise of that sort? Surely what we are talking about is not whether we should go out into the streets to round up 50,000 people, but whether we should release, or continue to detain, a much smaller number who are already in our prisons or hospitals.

Another rhetorical use of statistics is the argument that even if we released every man of violence as soon as he had served his just sentence, the resulting increase in crimes of intentional violence would be negligible. This is probably true. The great majority of people convicted of intentional crimes of violence not resulting in homicide are released after a few years; and the release of the remaining minority a few years earlier than they would otherwise have become free would add only a small percentage to the annual total of violent crimes. But this argument implies that because we cannot prevent the great majority of violent crimes we should not try to prevent a few of them. If we reasoned like this, we would never disqualify dangerous drivers.

What might worry us morally would be statistics showing that people whom we are detaining for the protection of others are no more likely to be violent in the future than the man in the street; more precisely, than any other member of the same sex and age-group who has not yet committed violence.[7] And there *are* one or two categories of violent offenders of whom this is probably true. An example is the parent who puts his or her children to death — intending perhaps to commit suicide as well — while he or she is in a severe depression; or the hitherto non-violent man who kills his wife, or mistress, out of justifiable jealousy. There is

---

[7] And if we had the necessary information we should, of course, add ethnic and occupational groups.

scope here for some very relevant research.

But with such exceptions it would be very difficult to argue that the violent people whom we are detaining are no more likely to commit further violence than hitherto non-violent people. In general the evidence strongly suggests, at least so far as males are concerned:

that each age-group has what we may call its own general probability of behaving with serious violence, which is quite low, though slightly higher for young adults than for older ones;

but that in each age-group the man who is known to have committed violence once already has a probability which is definitely higher than the general probability; and

that this probability increases somewhat with each additional known act of violence, although there is almost certainly a ceiling somewhere.

Truly 'nothing predicts behavior like behavior'.[8] In short, with the sort of exceptions I have instanced, it cannot be argued that the violent people whom we detain are no more likely to commit violence in the future than the non-violent man in the street.

NON-ARITHMETICAL RULES

But what sort of non-arithmetical rules would help in deciding when to apply purely protective measures? I can, as I promised, offer a few. They do not have the spurious precision of the arithmetic just discussed: in the last analysis they are an appeal to values.

1. The first is concerned with the sort of harm to which we should limit such measures. I suggest that when the measures involve serious and lasting hardship for the persons to whom we apply them — as any form of detention does — they

[8] W. C. Kvaraceus in *Anxious Youth.*

should be used only to prevent serious and lasting hardship to other individuals, of a kind which, once caused, cannot be remedied. Since most loss of or damage to property can be remedied by compensation,[9] whether by the offender, insurance, or the State, this rule excludes all or nearly all property offences (one can have an argument however about the theft or damage of unique works of art). It excludes temporary alarm (such as that caused by an imitation or unloaded pistol) and minor affronts to decency, such as exhibitionism. It *includes*, however, lasting psychological harm as well as disabling or disfiguring physical injury; so that rape, blackmail, kidnapping would be included. Nor does the rule insist that the harm must actually have been done; if the offender intended the harm or must have realised that it was a highly probable result of what he did or attempted, he should come within the rule.

2. The second rule is that there should be good reason to believe that the actions to which the first rule applies were not an isolated, out-of-character episode so far as the individual offender was concerned. Similar conduct on two or more occasions, separated by substantial periods of time, would be good reason to believe this; so would a declared intention, such as vengeance on the members of a family.

3. The third rule, however, is that if it can be reasonably argued that the circumstances which provided the offender with his incentive have ceased to exist (for example, through the death of his enemies), or that for some other reason (such as incapacity) he is unlikely to repeat his behaviour, this argument must operate in his favour. This rule will sound fairly uncontroversial, until I argue that it should also apply, though not invariably, to an offender's first experience of compulsory detention. In plain terms, if for the offence which brings him within the scope of Rule 1 the offender has

---

[9] I say 'remedied' rather than 'compensated' because there are kinds of harm for which compensation can be paid, but which are not thereby *remedied*: *e.g.*, the loss of a unique work of art.

been sentenced to imprisonment or otherwise compulsorily detained for the first time in his life, it can be reasonably argued that this experience will make him less likely to repeat his behaviour. Of course, there will be obvious exceptions; for instance, the man who after a year or two inside still says 'The first thing I'm going to do when I get out is to finish him off properly this time'. Again, someone who has already experienced imprisonment (or its equivalent) for some quite different behaviour, such as mere theft, would not benefit from this rule, which implies only that the first period of compulsory detention should not, for the sole purpose of protecting others, be made longer than it would otherwise have been.

4. The fourth rule is that if any less drastic measure than detention offers a reasonable prospect of protecting others, it should be used instead. In some cases supervision offers this prospect, especially when coupled with sensible requirements (such as residence at a specified address) or with prohibitions (for example, someone who has acted as an enforcer for a protection racket, and whose face is well known to the local police, could be forbidden to enter certain parts of a city). People could be disqualified from doing certain jobs — for instance, those involving responsibility for children. It is true that to some people the idea of strict supervision is objectionable, and not merely because of its practical difficulty. They regard it as too burdensome, or as incompatible with freedom. Most offenders, however, prefer conditional freedom to detention, even if they make things difficult for their supervisors. Doctrinaire objectors to strict supervision must face the fact that they are making it more difficult for courts to shorten prison sentences, or to consider non-custodial precautions, and more difficult for parole authorities to release dangerous offenders.

5. The fifth, and last, rule is that if you feel justified in detaining someone or prolonging his detention solely for the safety of others, the conditions of his detention should be made as tolerable as possible. The force of this rule, like that

of the others, is a moral one. When the detention is no longer justifiable as retribution, denunciation, deterrence or correction, but solely as a protection for others, its conditions should be no worse, apart from the deprivation of liberty, than those which a law-abiding wage-earner would enjoy outside. This is, of course, an idealistic standard to set, and there is scope here for a great deal of detailed discussion and ingenuity; all that can be stated here is the principle.

WHO SHOULD DECIDE WHAT?

Who is to apply these rules? To some extent the answer must vary according to the structure of a society's law enforcement system, and according to the degree of trust which its members have in their police, in their courts and their advisers, and in the administrators and staffs of their prisons and hospitals. Unless this trust is complete however – and it never should be – the limits of protective sentencing must be set by the legislature. The form of the sentence and the circumstances in which a person should be eligible for it are matters for legislation. On the other hand, legislation should not attempt to define circumstances in which a protective measure *must* be imposed; only circumstances in which it *may* be imposed. It should always be possible for a human being, whether acting as a sentencer or in some other capacity, to say 'The law allows a protective measure in this case, but it does not seem necessary'. Except where murder is concerned, most modern legislation takes this form.

The difficulties of drafting a legal definition of eligibility can be exaggerated, especially if one makes the mistake of trying to define the circumstances in which a protective measure *must* be used. As has just been said, the most that legislation should attempt is a definition of circumstances in which it *may* be used, leaving the sentencer or the psychiatric authority, as the case may be, the discretion *not* to use it. Once this approach is adopted, the difficulties diminish. It is not impossible to draw up a list of criminal offences to which protective measures should be restricted.[10] This is the solution adopted in several penal codes. It is not impossible to stipulate that evidence must be provided that there is a substantial probability that the offender will, if not prevented, behave in a similarly harmful way in the future. There are, of course, special legal problems in compulsory commitment to mental hospitals or juvenile institutions, especially where this can be arranged without the authority of a court; but one attractive solution would be to enact that nobody, whether adult or not, sane or not, can be detained solely for the protection of others without the express authority of a court, again requiring the court to be satisfied about the probability of future similar behaviour.

But is a court the best authority to exercise this discretion? I am not suggesting that we remove sentencing from the functions of criminal courts. What I have suggested elsewhere[11] is that a court which thinks it has a case for a protective sentence should not have the final say in the matter: only the power to remit the case to a special tribunal.[12] This would have two advantages. It would limit courts to the functions of sentencing for deterrent, corrective, even retributive or denunciatory purposes, thus making it clear that the protection of society is not the function of an ordinary sentence.[13]

Secondly, since the occasions on which a protective

[10] The more detailed the subdivisions of wrong-doing in the criminal code, the more effective this will be in excluding the sorts of behaviour against which we do not demand protection. Conversely, a vague code, which, for example, labelled as rape not only a violent assault on an unwilling woman but also intercourse with a girl just under the age of consent, will make such a list open to misuse.

[11] *Sentencing in a Rational Society.*

[12] It should be possible to appeal against the decision to remit the case to the tribunal.

[13] But when remitting the case, the court could indicate what sentence it would have imposed if the need for protecting others had not arisen.

sentence is justified are rare, so that few if any ordinary courts encounter enough of them to build up any experience worth the name, it would ensure that these cases come before an authority which would specialise in them, which could be given a set of guiding rules (not necessarily in statutory language) and which could both initiate research and apply its results. The tribunal would have power to decide on less drastic measures than detention in suitable cases. It should be clear that this proposal is based on the assertion not that courts are incompetent at sentencing, but that protective measures should be sharply distinguished from ordinary sentences.

THE FORM OF SENTENCE

It is the *form* of the custodial sentence, however, which arouses the sharpest disagreement. Not only anti-protectionists but even some people who accept the need for occasional sentences of protective length argue that it is unnecessary, or even undesirable, to legislate for a special kind of sentence. Unnecessary because, they argue, courts have sufficient scope, within the maxima set by law, to increase the length of a sentence with protection in view. Undesirable, because the existence of a special sentence would encourage courts to use it, as is said to have happened in the U.S.A. The argument that it is unnecessary holds only in jurisdictions where four conditions are fulfilled: high permissible maxima for all the relevant kinds of offences, express authority in statute or case-law to add to the normal length of a prison sentence in order to protect others, an obligation on sentencers to declare when they are using imprisonment in this way, and the possibility of appeals against such use. The argument that the existence of a special sentence would make it too popular with sentencers is not borne out by experience, or at least by experience in some countries. In Denmark the well thought-out and well-drafted revision of the *forvaring* (protective sentence) statutes did not lead to a marked increase in its use: indeterminate protective sentences are too unpopular there, as they are in Scandinavia as a whole. In England successive efforts to offer judges an extended form of sentence for persistent (not necessarily dangerous) offenders have failed: temporary enthusiasm for each new offer was followed by virtual disuse. The use of 'life' as a discretionary sentence for dangerous offenders has been strictly limited by English case-law — that is, judge-made law — to offenders who are mentally unstable.

In favour of a special form of sentence for the dangerous are two powerful considerations. It compels sentencers to make it clear when they are trying to protect the public. In England it is too easy for a judge to add a few years onto the prison term he would otherwise have chosen, so long as he keeps within the legal maximum and the normal range. He may or may not say expressly that he has done so in order to protect others: if he does not, it is very difficult to appeal against the sentence on the ground that it is unnecessarily protective. The second advantage is that a special protective sentence can have special provisions designed with dangerousness in view: an obvious example is after-care arrangements.

But the most important problem is clearly the method of selection of a release-date. How should this be done? This question is best approached indirectly, by asking easier questions first. At what stage should release be decided upon? Who should have the final say? The answers to these will at least exclude certain possible forms of sentence. For example, it is very difficult to argue that the exact duration of protective detention should be determined at the time of first sentencing. This makes sense only when the aim of a sentence is deterrence, denunciation, deserved punishment or correction.[14] When the aim is the protection of others, the date of

---

[14] It makes sense in the case of correction if it is recognised that correction which has not taken place within a certain period is unlikely to take place at all.

release must logically be determined at a later stage. Once this is recognised, the question whether the date should be determined by a court of law, or by some other agency becomes much more open to discussion. In countries with parole boards the function of deciding, or at least recommending, release dates usually falls to them; but both the theory and practice of parole are under attack these days. In France, some sentences are reviewable by a judge who is not the sentencing judge; but this system, too, is open to criticisms, of which the most obvious is that a single person, who is also a career judge, is not the best qualified or most objective of arbiters. If my proposal for a specialised authority were adopted, it would be desirable, though not logically necessary, to entrust it with this function.

If that proposal is rejected, however, an authority resembling a parole board seems preferable to a judicial authority. When the question at issue is not distributive justice, desert, denunciation or deterrence, but whether an offender is less likely than he was to do harm, what is needed are not legal qualifications, but a combination of several kinds of expertise. The chief criticism levelled against parole boards is that they tend to 'resentence' individuals on the basis of much the same information as was before the original sentencer. Whether this is so is very questionable; but even if it were true, we need not accept the implication that resentencing is necessarily a bad thing: some sentences are all the better for reconsideration when feelings have died down. But that is a digression: what we are considering is an entirely different sort of decision, to which the considerations involved in ordinary sentencing are to be irrelevant.

If this is granted, it seems to follow that a determinate sentence has little if anything to recommend it. If short, it may be too short, so that the staff of an institution have to release a man who is as dangerous as when he arrived. If long, it may be too long. Even if a long sentence carries a built-in possibility of release before the due date, the sheer length of it can have two undesirable results. One is that it may influence the releasing authority, the other is that it may demoralise the offender.

There are also objections to a completely indeterminate sentence, such as the 'life' sentence. It is said to be even more demoralising than a long determinate sentence, because it offers not even a distant guarantee of freedom. The extent to which this generalisation is justified must depend partly on the personality of the lifer himself, partly on what offenders believe to be the likely period of detention under such a sentence. In North America life sentences frequently mean 20 years inside; in Sweden the indeterminate protective sentence usually leads to conditional release within three or four years. In Britain lifers are usually released after eight, nine or ten years, but the period varies from one to twenty years at the extremes, so that a lifer who reaches his eighth or ninth year without being promised a release date is likely to become very anxious or depressed.

Complete indeterminacy is not the only alternative, however, to a so-called determinate sentence. One possibility is a sentence which must be reviewed at short intervals; a Canadian Bill adopted this solution. Two British committees — the Scottish Council on Crime and the Butler Committee on Mentally Abnormal Offenders — have recommended it. Its essential feature is the statutory insistence on regular review, at which the case for further detention, rather than the case for release, has to be made. It can also incorporate compulsory post-release supervision, again with regular review.

Another possibility — adopted in the Netherlands — is a renewable sentence. This would be a sentence of a length fixed in accordance with ordinary sentencing considerations, which was expressly subject to review not long before its termination, at which stage the reviewing body would be permitted to make a case to a court for a limited extension. If it did not make such a case, or if the court was not convinced by the case, the offender would automatically be released. This has the attraction that it makes detention

solely for public protection impossible without the continuing concurrence both of experts and of the judiciary.

Any solution — apart from one which simply rules out
protective sentencing — is open to the objection that it is
difficult for those who have charge of dangerous offenders
in conditions of captivity to tell, on the basis of hard facts,
whether a man is any less likely to repeat his harmful behaviour when he is not in captivity. The problem can be, and
sometimes is, exaggerated. There are cases in which changed
circumstances, attitudes or physical capacity clearly reduce
the likelihood of repetition. In any case, the problem can be
diminished by more flexible systems of provisional release
and by thorough investigation (and in some cases control) of
the conditions under which the offender will be living when
released. And since the problem is shared by all constructive
solutions it cannot be an objection to any of them.

DETENTION WITHOUT TRIAL

What I have been saying until now may have sounded as if
I had in mind only dangerous offenders who are tried and
sentenced. In fact I have not overlooked the problem of
compulsory commitment to mental hospitals without trial;
and my five rules are as applicable to them as to any convicted offender. Nevertheless, patients do pose two distinct
problems. One is the procedural question: how do we safeguard them against unwarranted detention beyond the stage
at which they cease to improve under treatment? The nature
and effectiveness of safeguards varies so much from one jurisdiction to another that detailed proposals could be worked
out only in each different context. But the general principle,
I suggest, must be that the need to detain any involuntary
patient beyond six months should be reviewed at regular
intervals[15] by some authoritative body of people who are all

---

[15] Without the necessity for an application by the patient.

completely independent of the hospital in which the patient is detained. (It should also be the function of that body to make sure that any long-term patient who is said to be a voluntary inmate really is voluntary.) The reviewing members should include a lawyer, a social worker, and a psychiatrist. The member whose position will be most difficult will, of course, be the psychiatrist, because the cohesiveness of his profession will sometimes mean that a decision to order release will be embarrassing for him. In order to lessen this difficulty, the decision should be by a confidential vote, so that his colleagues need not know whether he voted for or against it; and there should always be enough non-psychiatrists to outvote the psychiatrists.

There would be some advantages in the proposal that a person regarded as dangerous should always be prosecuted, so that what he has actually done could be subjected to the thorough scrutiny of a criminal court. Even the Butler Committee in England, which recommended that the prosecution of the mentally disordered should be avoided unless there were strong reasons for it, expressly said that dangerousness is a strong reason. But while this is a fairly sound principle, it would not solve some problems. In particular, it would not deal with the patient who has not actually done or attempted anything that could have resulted in serious harm, but has merely talked about doing it. An example which is bound to occur to everyone is the paranoid man who regards the head of State or some other important person as the source of his persecution, and who says that if the persecution does not stop he will kill him. In many jurisdictions he would have committed no criminal offence. It is all very well to compel him to enter hospital for treatment; but what do we do when the psychiatrists have done their best by way of therapy, and the only justification for further detention is that he might still do what he has talked of doing? Should we release him and keep an eye on him to see whether he tries to acquire a firearm or manufacture a letter-bomb? Should we detain him on the grounds that someone who talks about killing presents a sufficient danger? The only solution seems to me to be a reviewing authority of the kind I have been describing.[16]

Having argued throughout this chapter that it is defensible from the moral point of view to detain, or otherwise control, certain people for the protection of others, and that from the legal point of view it is not impossible to draft provisions for this purpose with satisfactory safeguards, I want to redress the balance with two final points. One is that so far as this problem is concerned no system of rules can avoid the need for decisions by human beings, with all their biases and irrational fears. The other is that custodial institutions, however liberally managed, are places of last resort, whether for the mentally ill or for offenders. There are a few people so handicapped that they find institutional life more tolerable than what we call 'life in the community'; and then it is usually because they have no community, or none that will accept them. But with these exceptions, to dispose of someone in this way is to deprive him of much that makes life worth living. Almost any degree of non-custodial control is preferable.

SUMMARY

The main points I have been making are these. The difficulties of defining dangerousness have been exaggerated: we do it in practice every day. The objections to labelling people as dangerous are no greater than the objections to labelling them 'loyal' or 'deceitful'. What is debatable is

[16] In England, a compulsorily detained patient who is not subject to a restriction order imposed by a criminal court can apply to the local Mental Health Review Tribunal. The Tribunal *must* direct his release if satisfied that he is not suffering from mental illness, psychopathic disorder or subnormality *or* that, even if he is, continued detention is not necessary in the interests of his health or safety or for the protection of others (Mental Health Act, 1959, c. 72, s. 123).

what we are justified in doing to dangerous people by way of incapacitation; and what particularly needs justification in the case of offenders is their detention for longer than other penal aims require. But to condemn this as punishing people for crimes not yet committed is an oversimplification. The arithmetical arguments of the anti-protectionists are also rhetorical rather than sound. On the other hand, the use of detention to incapacitate the dangerous offender should be subject to five rules.

The difficulties of drafting legislation can also be exaggerated, especially if it is assumed that the law should try to define circumstances in which special sentences *must* be imposed. All it should attempt is to set fairly strict limits to the use of such a sentence. The decision to use it or not in a given case should ideally be taken by a special tribunal to which courts could refer *prima facie* cases: this would have several advantages. As for the form which the sentence should take, there are strong objections both to sentences of fixed length and completely indeterminate detention. These are not, however, the only possibilities: others are the reviewable and the renewable sentence.

The detention of mentally disordered offenders for the sake of others raises one special problem. A rule that this should never be done without prosecution — that is, never under civil procedure — would prevent most abuses. An awkwardness is the rare case in which a disordered person seems to be talking seriously about killing (or seriously harming) others. Apart from the anti-protectionist's course — to do nothing — all that can be done to prevent undue detention in such cases is to have them reviewed frequently by a competent authority.

The most important rule of all, however, is that detention is a last resort: any kind of non-custodial measure, however much of a nuisance, should be considered first.

6 Mitigating and aggravating

This is one of the least discussed aspects of sentencing, at least amongst Anglo-American lawyers and penologists. Only one text-book in English devotes more than a few paragraphs to it: David Thomas' *Principles of Sentencing*, which has a whole chapter on mitigation.

It is possible to distinguish three approaches to the problem by penal codes. What might be called the Continental approach, since it is found in many countries influenced by the Code Napoleon, is to specify in statute the aspects of an offence which the sentencer can take into account in reducing or increasing the severity of the penalty, sometimes indicating a minimum penalty if a particular aggravation is present (as Greece does for ringleaders of riots). If an aggravating or mitigating feature is present, it *must* be taken into account, although in practice the arithmetic of the reasoning is difficult to assess, especially when both mitigating and aggravating circumstances are present. Perhaps for this reason, appeals based on aggravation or mitigation are not often successful, the appellate courts tending to regard such reasoning as best done by the court which tried the case.[1]

Another approach is to sub-divide offences by definitions of the more and the less serious forms of them. The obvious example is the American device of distinguishing 'degrees' of murder, with different maximum or mandatory penalties. A similar American expedient is to call some ways of committing an offence a mere 'misdemeanour', while others

[1] See for example the paper by E. Dreher at the 9th International Congress on Penal Law, 1964. *Excerpta Criminologica* (1965) has interesting summaries of this and other papers describing the solutions adopted by various countries.

are 'felonies' carrying more serious penalties. This does not prevent judges from varying non-mandatory penalties according to other mitigating or aggravating criteria. A recent development in a few States, however, called 'flat rate' or 'fixed time' sentencing, prescribes by statute the term of imprisonment which is the standard penalty for each felony, and restricts increases or reductions for mitigating or aggravating circumstances to one or two years. Because appeal against sentence is a comparatively recent development in the U.S.A. it has not been the subject of a critical survey on the lines of Thomas' book. Some years ago, however, the Twentieth Century Fund's Task Force on Criminal Sentencing, in its Report *Fair and Certain Punishment*, listed the aggravating circumstances which seemed to be widely recognised by American judges. For some reason it did not give a list of mitigating circumstances, although it listed its own recommendations. It may well have had difficulty in compiling such a list, since aggravation is a commoner theme than mitigation amongst American sentencers.

The reverse is certainly the case in England, where there is very little in the way of statutory attempts to deal with the problem, and a great deal is left to sentencers' discretion. In a few instances the law distinguishes a more serious form of an offence, with a higher maximum penalty. 'Aggravated burglary' is burglary committed with a weapon of offence, for which the maximum is 'life' instead of 10 years. Sexual intercourse with a girl under 13 is a more serious offence than with one between her 13th and 16th birthdays. As for mitigation, the only statutory examples are even fewer. The law distinguishes between murder, manslaughter, infanticide and child destruction. There are general restrictions on types of custodial penalty for offenders under 21 and other lower age-limits. Otherwise it is left to the judge to decide whether some feature of the case justifies him in severity or leniency. The Court of Appeal's influence is considerable, but one-sided. If the judge expressly increases the penalty for some reason, and the defendant appeals, it can uphold or disagree with the judge's reasoning. If he refuses to take into account a mitigating feature, an appeal may persuade it to say that he was wrong. But the prosecution does not bring forward reasons for greater severity, and cannot appeal against a sentence which it privately considers too lenient (as it can do in Canada, for example). Nor can there ever be an appeal on the grounds that the sentencer should *not* have mitigated the penalty for this or that reason. For this, and perhaps other less tangible reasons, English courts, including the appellate court, are 'mitigation-minded'. It is not much of an exaggeration, as I shall show, to say that the normal English sentence for a given type of offence is what is imposed on a man in good health and the prime of life, with a substantial previous record of convictions, no dependants, no pardonable temptation or provocation, and no demonstrable remorse or other redeeming attributes. From that starting point the sentencer tends to work downward rather than upward, considering any reasonable argument by the defence in favour of leniency, but seldom considering − because nobody is in a position to argue them − reasons for greater severity.

CONSISTENCY

An example is the reduction of sentences with the sole aim of being consistent. The best example is that of Reeves.[2] He and another man had been convicted of receiving 20 stolen pitch-fibre pipes. The other man chose summary trial (wisely as it turned out), and was fined £25 (this was in 1963). Reeves, on the other hand, chose trial by jury, and was sentenced to 9 months' imprisonment. The Court of Criminal Appeal did not consider his sentence excessive: on the contrary they thought the other man's fine too lenient. But

[2] (1964) Crim. L. R., 67.

their respect for consistency obliged them to reduce Reeves' sentence by an amount which secured his immediate release from prison.

It is respect for consistency which has led to American demands for flat-rate sentencing. There is such a thing however, as pseudo-consistency, which simply looks to the legal classification of the offence and ignores real differences between instances. For many years the *Sunday Express* in Britain carried a column by 'John Gordon' which ridiculed courts by contrasting a severe sentence imposed by one court for, say, a fraud with a lenient one imposed by another on the same charge. Differences in circumstances, or in offenders' histories or motives, were ignored.

At the other extreme seems to be the Ontario Court of Appeal, which has not only rejected as irrelevant the sentences imposed on accomplices, but went as far as to declare that 'It is difficult, if not impossible, to reconcile the sentence in one case with the sentences in other cases. The Court must strive to its utmost to see that a sentence imposed upon a guilty person is appropriate to the particular circumstances of his case. It ... affords little assistance to the Court to know what sentences have been passed in other countries or jurisdictions or by other courts ...'.[3] It is true that few courts have regard to the sentencing policy of other countries; but the denial of the relevance of sentences in other jurisdictions (sc., in the same country) and other courts (sc., in the same jurisdiction) is remarkably uncompromising.[4]

[3] See *R. v. Simpson* (1956) 114 C.C.C. 152 (Ont. C. A.) and *R. v. Connor and Hall* (1957) 118 C.C.C. 237 (Ont. C. A.).

[4] The English Court of Appeal (Criminal Division) understandably refuses to take into account sentences not considered on appeal: see for example *Hayes and Reidy* (1976) 63 Cr. App. R. 292, but takes some pains to achieve consistency in its own sentencing policy. The occasional case in which it rejects comparisons with *all* other sentences should not be taken too seriously: see Thomas's comments on *R. v. Rees* (1978) Crim. L. R. at 299.

Yet even this court did not reject the idea of consistency with its own sentences: an omission which can hardly have been *per incuriam.*[5] Even the most solipsist of courts must have in mind some sort of consistency. Yet this at once raises the question 'Consistency in respect of what?' The rule 'Treat like cases alike' means nothing unless it tells you what are relevant similarities. Age? Harm done? Motive?

The object of this chapter is not to consider all the grounds on which mitigation or aggravation have been or could be based. Some of them are of little interest: an example is extreme cruelty in the commission of an offence. What is of real interest is the underlying reasoning and its relationship to retributive, denunciatory or reductive aims. As I hope to show, courts sometimes take into account considerations which, though at first sight persuasive, have little if anything to do with these aims; and a question to which I shall return at the end of the chapter is whether this invalidates such considerations or not.

JUSTIFYING AIMS OF PENALTIES

Mitigation and aggravation are notions which properly belong to the retributive approach to penalties. Someone who regards retribution either as his justifying aim or as a principle which sets an upper limit to penalties inspired by other aims can — indeed must, unless he is a very primitive kind of punisher — hold that the circumstances of individual cases will sometimes justify increases or decreases in the normal penalties (or limits to penalties, as the case may be). A denouncer, on the other hand, must find it less easy to accommodate the idea of individual variations in severity. His aim is to express disapproval of the offence by a penalty which will convey this to his public. It is true (as I have pointed out in Chapter 2) that in order to succeed in this he

[5] *i.e.,* due to inadvertence, though it sounds better in lawyers' Latin.

must have regard to his public's idea of what is a retributively appropriate punishment, if his penalty is not to be rejected as inadequate or harsh; so that when the public's knowledge or beliefs about an individual case enhance or diminish its gravity he may well adjust his penalty accordingly, and even perhaps explain his reasons publicly. Nevertheless, he is in effect being influenced by retributive reasoning, even if it is not his own reasoning.

EXEMPLARY SENTENCES

Leniency and severity can occasionally, however, be inspired by reductive aims. Courts sometimes impose what in England is called an 'exemplary sentence': that is, one which is intentionally more severe than the penalty which would be normal in the circumstances, in order to deter potential imitators. This is sometimes done when a serious offence is thought to be increasing in prevalence.

It is in fact doubtful whether an occasional sentence of exceptional severity is at all likely to have a general deterrent effect. The evidence in favour is anecdotal, and when examined is found to be far from conclusive. Thus it is often said that an outbreak of attacks on coloured people in the Notting Hill district of London in the late summer of 1958 was suppressed by the sentencing of nine youths to 4 years' imprisonment. Since all but one were admitted by the prosecution to be 'of good character' these were said to be exceptionally severe sentences, although the Court of Appeal did not agree. However, that may be, it is very doubtful whether they had the deterrent effect claimed. In fact the attacks seemed to have been prompted by the appearance of an inflammatory racialist broadsheet, and may have died down because a document of that sort has only a temporary effect. Certainly there were instances of racial violence in Notting Hill not long *after* the 4-year sentences. There was also increased police activity. Finally, the nine imprisoned youths may have been the ring-leaders.

The best study known to me of the general deterrent effect of an exceptionally severe sentence was carried out by the Home Office Research Unit after a Birmingham youth had been sentenced to 20 years for a particularly brutal mugging in 1973. Because of its severity, the sentence was well publicised in the national as well as the local press.Yet when the week-by-week frequencies of muggings during that summer in Birmingham and two comparable cities, Liverpool and Manchester, were studied it was found that there was no decrease in the weeks following the sentence.[6]

On the whole the English Court of Appeal does not approve exemplary sentences, but not so much because it is sceptical of their efficacy as because it values consistency.

Sentencers' faith in the efficacy of exemplary prison sentences contrasts oddly with their use of fines, especially in English magistrates' courts. Amounts are usually chosen with an eye to consistency (the so-called 'tariff system'). Any departure from the tariff is almost always in the downward direction, in order to take account of the offender's relative poverty or heavy financial burdens. It is rare for the amount to be increased, even when the offender is so obviously wealthy that the usual fine can be no deterrent, only as it were a tax. This one-sided approach was criticised by the Wootton Committee in 1970, who said in effect that courts should be as ready to go above the tariff in such cases as they were to go below it. The Lord Chancellor confirmed that this would not be improper; but lay magistrates — and

---

[6] See Baxter and Nuttall (1975). Similarly, the Recorder of Birmingham claimed in 1965 to have discouraged an outbreak of theft and damage in telephone kiosks by severe sentences; but a study of the figures by Thomas showed that this was an over-simplification. It is more likely that the reduction in such offences was due to the increased surveillance of the police (see the *Birmingham Mail* of 4 October 1965). I am indebted to David Thomas for his unpublished graphs.

their clerks — are still unconvinced of this.[7] The result makes no sense either from a retributive or from a reductive point of view. The same fine cannot represent proportionate punishment for people with widely different disposable incomes; nor can it have the same deterrent influence.

Strictly speaking, however, the notions of aggravation and mitigation belong, as has been pointed out, not to the reductive but to the retributive approach: more precisely, to that form of retributivism which holds that the choice and severity of penalties should be proportional[8] to culpability.[9] In the great majority of cases in which sentencers regard an offence as mitigated or aggravated they are reasoning that the offender's blameworthiness is in some way diminished or enhanced. Even sentencers who would argue that the main aim of a tariff of penalties is deterrent, and therefore reductive, are at the same time prepared to argue in individual cases that the penalty should be less or more severe than the tariff suggests, not because this would have the same deterrent effect but because for retributive reasons the normal penalty seems too severe or not severe enough.

This sounds straightforward enough: but its complications will soon become apparent. For there are two sorts of reason for increasing or reducing the normal penalty. One is that the offender seems less or more culpable than most of those found guilty of similar offences. The other is that in his circumstances the normal penalty would inflict more hardship than it does on most offenders (or less hardship, of course, though sentencers rarely reason thus). It is the latter logic which reduces a poor man's fine, although — as we have just seen — English courts are reluctant to increase the rich man's fine. Since there are no technical terms — at least in English

---

[7] An interesting exception is the fining of foreign shoplifters by London Magistrates (usually stipendiary — that is, full-time paid — magistrates), who have been imposing fines of £1,000 or more on shoplifting tourists from abroad who had enough money in their wallets!

[8] In cruder versions, 'commensurate with' (see p. 38).

[9] In cruder versions, 'the harm done'.

— which distinguish these two modes of reasoning, I shall call the first 'culpability-based' and the second 'suffering-based'.

AGE

It is suffering-based reasoning, for example, which induces sentencers to shorten the normal prison sentence for the elderly offender: according to Thomas this is likely after the age of 60 in the English Court of Appeal. Otherwise, says the court, he would have to spend too large a fraction of the rest of his life in captivity. Similar reasoning sometimes leads to reduced terms for younger offenders whose life-expectancy is short. But this is not carried to the logical extreme of conceding smaller reductions to healthy offenders who are in their fifties or forties. If it were, we might have quite complicated calculations, starting with the assumption that the normal sentence is appropriate for a man of, say, 25, and that the offender will live for three score years and ten (or indeed until the average age of death for an overweight heavy smoker, or whatever he is). A ready reckoner would then tell the sentencer how many months to deduct for a man of, say 43. If this is regarded as a *reductio ad adsurdum*, why?

In fact, English sentencers seem to feel a need to reduce terms of imprisonment at the other end of the adult age-range too. Thomas says that this has been done in England not only for offenders who are under 21, but even for a few who are under 30. This is an unofficial echo of the statutory protection from the full penalty which juveniles enjoy: a protection which some codes extend in an attenuated form to the 'young adult' age-group. It originated in the presumption that children do not fully appreciate the nature, consequences or wrongness of their illegal acts: an example of culpability-based reasoning. As the protection was successively advanced, however, to higher and higher ages it became more and more obviously a fiction; and where offenders in their late 'teens are concerned it would be sounder to adopt suffering-based reasoning and argue that to spend part of one's youth in prison is worse than spending part of one's middle age there. Perhaps some sentencers and the Court of Appeal do reason thus: it certainly seems more realistic and consistent.

The American Task Force's approach to the relevance of age, however, is culpability-based, with one odd exception. It actually mentions the offender's 'relative youth' as a factor which may *aggravate* when it suggests that he is a future danger: a reductive argument.[10] Not that it endorses this view: in its own recommendations youth or old age are mitigating circumstances, but only when as a result the offender 'lacked substantial judgment in committing the offence'. There is no trace of suffering-based reasoning either here or in any other recommendation of the Task Force.

IGNORANCE OF THE LAW

In strict legal theory, ignorance of the law excuses nobody. Honest lawyers admit that this principle is dictated by expediency: if ignorance of the law were an acceptable excuse it would be too hard for the prosecution to counter it by proving that the offender did in fact know that what he was doing was illegal. In one or two jurisdictions, however, it is conceded by the courts that a man's ignorance, especially in the case of a new regulatory offence, may entitle him to an acquittal: Norway is an example. In Anglo-American practice sentencers, though debarred from accepting it as an excuse, can accept it as a plea in mitigation because of their wide discretion. In 1978 a man was convicted at Portsmouth Crown Court of trying to recruit men for the Rhodesian

---

[10] There is a trace of similar reasoning by an English judge in the case of *Storey* (1973) 57 Cr. App. R at 847.

army and air force. He had been unsuccessful, but the judge's main reason for letting him off with a conditional discharge was that the police evidence confirmed his plea that he did not know that he was contravening regulations.[11] This is culpability-based reasoning. Whether it would be approved by the Court of Appeal is uncertain. Even Canadian courts, though sceptical of most pleas in mitigation, have been influenced by legal ignorance. A judge acquitted a go-go dancer in Manitoba of taking part in an immoral performance, with remarks which gave one of her colleagues the impression that she could give a similar performance with impunity. The second dancer's sentence was reduced on appeal, even though the court thought that 'no reasonable person could find, in the remarks of Riley J., justification for some of the things that this lady has done'.[12]

MORAL BOOK-KEEPING

There is a whole group of considerations which can be called 'retributive' only by a stretch of meaning, and which really ought to be sharply distinguished. Sentencers sometimes reduce the penalties for an offender because of some meritorious action of his which has nothing to do with the offence, or indeed with any past or future offences. Men have had prison terms shortened because they have had good war records (a quarter of a century before!) have saved boys from drowning, or have given their sisters kidneys. This makes sense only if:

a. offenders are being sentenced for their total moral worth rather than the offence of which they stand convicted;

and b. their moral worth can be calculated by moral book-keeping of this crude sort, in which spectacular behaviour counts more than unobtrusive decency.

[11] *Daily Telegraph*, 7th May 1978.
[12] (1973) 10 C.C.C. (2d.) at p. 36 (Man. Dist. Ct.).

It is most unlikely that any judge would assent to either of these propositions if they were put to him: yet judges do reason in this way, as if they were somewhat sentimental Recording Angels. I must add, however, that I have come across no case in which a judge *increased* a man's sentence because he had evaded conscription, let a swimmer drown or refused his sister a kidney: that would undoubtedly be censured by the Court of Appeal. The most that could be said is that in English courts it can do a man harm if, when he is being sentenced for theft, the judge is told, say, that he spends all his money on drink or gambling.

CRIMINAL RECORDS

This brings us to the stage at which it is possible to consider the universally approved practice of taking a man's record of previous offences into account, whether in the crude ways proposed by the Task Force and the authors of *Doing Justice* or in the sophisticated ways of the English Court of Appeal. This can − sometimes at least − be justified by a reductive argument: if his record shows that he is undeterred by fines or short prison sentences, it is logical to see whether a prison sentence, or a longer one, will do the trick. The Task Force were even prepared to see sentences increased beyond the 'presumptive' (*i e,* tariff) level in such cases, a line which strongly suggests that their reasoning was reductive:

> 'The theory behind this approach is that sentences for first offenders should be relatively low but that they should increase − rather sharply − with each prior conviction ...'

This can hardly be called a theory, since it does not explain why the sentence should increase, let alone why it should do so rather sharply; but sharp increases suggest a deterrent justification.

Doing Justice, on the other hand, puts forward a clear retributive case:

> 'The reason for treating the first offense as less serious is ... that repetition alters the degree of culpability that may be attributed to the offender. In assessing a first offender's culpability, it ought to be borne in mind that he was, at the time he committed the crime, only one of a large audience to whom the law impersonally addressed its prohibitions. His first conviction, however, should call dramatically and personally to his attention that the behavior is condemned. A repetition of the offense following that conviction may be regarded as more culpable, since he persisted in the behavior after having been forcefully censured for it through his prior punishment'.

Given its premises, this argument certainly justifies an increase in the severity of the penalty for an offender's *second* offence. What it does not seem to justify are the subsequent increases for the third, etc., offence which *Doing Justice* in fact proposes.

The English Court of Appeal is not quite so explicit about its reasoning:

> 'Men are not sentenced on their records. They are sentenced for their offences ...'.

This seems very clear: a man's record is irrelevant. But in the next breath they add:

> '... If they have got bad records nothing can be taken off by way of mitigation, while if they have not got bad records a great deal can be taken off ...'.[13]

[13] *R. v. Bowman, Murphy and Bromwell* (1973) transcript 1543/B/72, cit. Thomas (1979).

This does not seem to be based on the argument used in *Doing Justice*: if it were, the important distinction would be between the man who has any record and the man who has none. (It is true that other cases show that first offenders do receive special consideration from the Court of Appeal, but apparently only as extreme cases of men without *bad* records.) Is it possible that the Court is once again resorting to moral book-keeping, and using previous records as an index of total moral worth? This interpretation is contradicted by the way in which similar previous offences are distinguished from dissimilar previous offences; moral book-keeping would regard most sorts of conviction as indications of wickedness. On the other hand, it is supported by the way in which the Court of Appeal is favourably impressed if there has been a substantial lapse of time between the present conviction and the last (unless of course the time has been spent 'inside'). It takes this as a sign that the offender has been trying to mend his ways. But *Doing Justice* also commends the doctrine that the longer the lapse of time the less relevant the previous conviction, and suggests that after a certain time the record should be wiped clean. Exactly why this should be done they do not explain. If their line of reasoning were consistent it would have to argue that after a certain time the offender might have forgotten the warning conveyed by his first punishment.

Do these theoretical ambiguities matter very much if — as seems to be the case — there is a considerable measure of agreement about the way in which records should be taken into account in practice? Unfortunately, they do matter. This is the feature of sentencing policy which offenders themselves most resent.[14] They agree with the Court of Appeal that men should be sentenced for their offences and not their records; but the courts seem to be doing the opposite. If, as not infrequently happens, A and B are sentenced

---

[14] I base this on regular discussions over more than ten years with mixed classes of prisoners and university students.

for the same offence, but B gets a longer term than A because
of a worse record, then – offenders argue – he is to some
extent being punished twice for his previous offences.[15] The
resentment is even greater if it is simply A's luck or skill,
and not his virtue, which explains his clean record.

The Court of Appeal's answer is apparently that B is not
being sentenced for his previous offences. He is getting the
appropriate sentence for his present one, but would not have
done if his record had been clean.[16] Yet this seems to imply
that the appropriate sentence for a given offence is more
accurately defined as the appropriate one for that offence
when committed by a person with previous convictions, or
at least similar previous convictions. It is very difficult to see
how this implication can be avoided: and it belongs to
moral book-keeping rather than to the strictly retributive
approach.

PLEADING GUILTY

There is a similar awkwardness in the distinction which
courts draw between offenders who plead guilty and those
who plead not guilty. Both in the U.S.A. and in England
(with the approval of the Court of Appeal) a guilty plea
often earns a lighter sentence.[17] The same is true of other
ways in which offenders may co-operate with the courts or

[15] It makes it worse if the Court of Appeal then reduces B's sentence
to equal A's and gives as its reason 'consistency', or its desire to remove
a grievance. Why should the principle of consistency operate in this
way only between partners in crime?

[16] Unless there were aggravating circumstances which outweighed
the mitigating effect of a clean record: see Thomas.

[17] Even in inquisitorial systems in which the judge has to inquire
into a crime which the offender admits, he is allowed to treat a con-
fession as mitigating behaviour if satisfied that it was made from
worthy motives. Conversely, obdurate lying in the teeth of the evidence can aggravate the sentence because of the light which it seems
to throw on his personality.

the police to save time or trouble or help in the conviction of other offenders. This makes sense if the justification is pure expediency: it is bargain justice at its most hard-headed. But it implies that the appropriate (or 'tariff' or 'presumptive') sentence for the offence is not simply that which is proportionate to culpability but that which is appropriate to the culpability of an offender who pleads not guilty and is otherwise unco-operative. And since courts distinguish between offenders who plead not guilty because they have a defence that is worth a try and those who insist on a trial without a worthwhile defence, even this statement needs refining.

REMORSE

Pleading guilty, however, is sometimes interpreted by the court as one of the signs of remorse. 'It is ... of course proper to give a man a lesser sentence if he has shown genuine remorse, amongst other things by pleading guilty'.[18] It is obviously not easy to be sure what are genuine signs of remorse and what are merely the tactics of an intelligent defendant or counsel. An embezzler's counsel is often able to say that his client has repaid all or most of what he stole; but such repayments usually begin after detection. Sincerity apart however, the justification for mitigating sentences to take account of remorse requires more than a moment's thought. The reasoning may simply be that his remorse shows that he has the right moral attitude; if so, the reasoning is either reductive or another example of moral bookkeeping. It might on the other hand be suffering-based, the implication being that the remorseful offender is already punishing himself to some extent. If so, remorse would have to be fairly powerful in order to qualify.

[18] *R. v. Harper* [1967] 3 All E. R. 617; 52 Cr. App. R. 21.

'NATURAL PUNISHMENT'

Whether remorse can be regarded as self-punishment or not, courts sometimes take into account the harm which a person's offence has done to him. A man whose bad driving has led to his own serious injury, or the death or injury of close relatives is sometimes penalised more leniently. Such reasoning is very ancient: one of the Roman reasons for not punishing madmen was that they were punished enough by their madness, and there have been echoes of this amongst English jurists.[19] Modern Continental jurists sometimes use the term *poena naturalis*: a 'natural' penalty. The West German Penal Code has an express provision (s.60) allowing courts, where the appropriate penalty does not exceed a year's imprisonment, not to impose it at all if the crime has such serious results for the offender that the imposition of the penalty would clearly fail in its objectives; an example being a case in which a motorist's negligence caused the death of his own wife as well as the wife of another driver.[20] Canadian courts seem to follow a tougher principle. Two parents whose children perished while left alone in their burning home received a suspended sentence. The Crown appealed, and the Manitoba Court of Appeal substituted 4 months' imprisonment, on the grounds that the sorrow of the defendants was not sufficient punishment.

On a strict interpretation of retributive punishment they were right. Punishment is something deliberately inflicted by order of the proper authority, not some natural consequence, intended or unintended, of the transgression itself. Yet, while it is a mistake to talk of 'natural punishment', I have pointed out that 'suffering-based reasoning' can consistently lead even punishers to mitigate the normal penalty

[19] See my *Crime and Insanity in England*, Vol. I.
[20] OLG Gelle: N.J.W. 1971, p. 575. I am indebted to Dr. Barbara Huber for drawing my attention to this and other features of the West German Penal Code.

in cases in which special circumstances — such as a short life-expectancy — would mean that it entailed more than usual suffering for the offender. It is only a slight extension of such reasoning to argue that grief-stricken husbands or parents would suffer excessively from imprisonment. What is less easy to justify is the West German proviso which restricts this ground of mitigation to short terms of imprisonment and makes it an all-or-nothing decision. It would be more consistent to allow courts to reduce a fine or prison term of any amount by any amount, at their discretion.

PROFESSIONALISM

A circumstance which sentencers seem to regard as especially aggravating is professionalism. As in sport, the amateur is judged by less exacting standards.[21] The interesting question is whether the courts' dislike of the professional is completely consistent with the strictly retributive doctrine that a man is sentenced for his offence and not for his record. Sometimes courts are really distinguishing between motives: an illegal abortion is more likely to be punished severely if the operator is shown to have asked for a large fee than if he or she seems to have done it out of pity or helpfulness. In other cases, however, the reasoning requires closer examination. I suspect — though a clear-cut example is hard to find — that if two men with no previous convictions were being sentenced for otherwise similar burglaries, the one who used professional tools would receive a more severe sentence.

---

[21] And, as in sport again, the line between the amateur and the professional is becoming hard to draw. Is a garage mechanic who burgles in his spare time a professional or an amateur? In fact, it is signs of competence and experience on which police and courts often base the distinction.

MOTIVES

In the common-law countries – and some others – the motive for an offence is something which a sentencer may take into account if he sees fit. In other countries – for instance West Germany – he is obliged to do so. In either case, there are mitigating motives and aggravating ones. Revenge is sweet, but wicked: mercy-killing presumptuous but pardonable. Hunger excites sympathy, withdrawal symptoms disgust. When sentences are varied in such circumstances the reasoning is moral and retributive. The only important problem arises when the sentencer has to deal with an offender from another culture with different moral attitudes toward certain motives. Vindication of family honour is regarded more or less as a duty in some societies: but should a British sentencer take this into account? If he is truly trying to assess culpability he should; and it is not unheard of for an English judge to do so. He may, however, argue that his duty is to uphold the moral values of his own society, and therefore to disregard outlandish codes of conduct. He may be torn between the feeling that he really ought to take them into account and the fear that if he does he will expose himself and his colleagues to all sorts of forensic folk-lore.

LAPSE OF TIME

'Lapse of time is no bar to the Crown' wrote Coke. Since his day even English legislators and courts have retreated some distance from his uncompromising standpoint. 'Statutes of limitations' have been applied to a few indictable offences – such as unlawful carnal knowledge of girls between their 13th and 16th birthdays – and to nearly all offences which are punishable on summary conviction. Many other countries apply time-limits much more widely: West Germany has various limits – ranging from 1 to 30 years – for all offences except genocide. Even when there is no limit a considerable lapse of time since the commission or discovery of the offence is sometimes accepted by a court as a mitigating feature. The justifications however for conferring impunity or mitigating penalties are worth a little discussion. One important argument is that after a considerable time the memory of witnesses cannot be trusted, witnesses who might assist the defendant may be dead or impossible to trace, and other evidence may be equally inaccessible. This is often a sound reason for not prosecuting; but when it is a matter of sentencing a properly convicted offender the arguments must be different.

Courts sometimes reduce the penalty when there has been unavoidable delay between detection and prosecution, so that the offender has already suffered suspense.[22] They particularly dislike cases in which police or prosecutors delay the bringing forward of charges until the defendant has completed, or nearly completed, a prison term for another offence, and will modify their sentences accordingly. English courts went a step further at the end of the nineteenth century,[23] and gradually adopted a practice whereby a defendant who is being sentenced for an offence can protect himself against such expedients by asking the sentencer to 'take into consideration' any number of similar offences with which he has not yet been charged. If the court agrees to do so it may add a little to the length of the appropriate prison term or fine, and he cannot then be prosecuted for those offences. The justification is the desire to give the offender a chance, after he has served one prison sentence, to show whether he can refrain from further crime.

Avoidable delay in prosecuting a detected offender, however, is a different thing from unavoidable delay in detecting

---

[22] In West Germany it has been held that avoidable delay of this sort violates Article 6 of the European Convention on Human Rights, which concerns the right to a speedy trial. By a compromise, however, the defendant can still receive a sentence, though it must be lighter than the one which he would otherwise have been given.

[23] See Margrave-Jones (1959).

or catching a culprit. It is sometimes argued that if in the interval he has behaved well this should count in his favour. Certainly it might convince the reducer that there was nothing to be gained from penalising him. A denouncer would be less happy; and a punisher might object that the lapse of time makes no difference to the need for retribution. It is true that, if the offender has meantime suffered from anxiety or remorse, suffering-based reasoning could take the interval into account. If on the other hand he experienced no such feelings, it is hard to see its relevance for the punisher.

It is sometimes said that 'the offender may have become a different moral being' (Stallybrass, 1945). This may simply be a metaphorical and overstated way of saying that he might be no longer psychologically capable of committing the crime, in which case there would be no reductive reason − apart from the publicity − for penalising him. It sounds, however, as if it is more than a metaphor: a claim that in a sense we would, after all this time, be punishing the wrong person. If all that is meant is that he must now be remorseful, that is something which suffering-based reasoning allows a punisher to take into account irrespective of the lapse of time. Perhaps what is meant is that the longer the interval the more likely he is to be remorseful; but as a general assumption this is very questionable indeed.

So far as I know nobody has claimed that the mere lapse of time weakens 'desert'. On the retributive view of punishment it is equally deserved a day or a year or ten years after the offence. A denouncer might argue that if the crime has been forgotten the need to symbolise disapproval of it has gone. Denouncers, however, are more inclined to maintain that the public needs to be reminded of the gravity of the crime: hence the exemption of genocide from the West German statutes of limitation.

THE FORGIVING VICTIM

Particularly interesting is the way in which some courts — including the English Court of Appeal — are sometimes willing to lighten a sentence if the victim indicates forgiveness. This cannot be based on retributive reasoning, since it has no bearing on either the offender's culpability or the degree of suffering involved. In certain circumstances it could be an indication of the offender's moral worth: a common situation is one in which a wife who has been assaulted by her husband says that she is willing to take him back. In such cases the court might argue that she knows him best and regards him as essentially a tolerable person. It might argue, on reductive lines, that if she is the only likely victim of his violence, and if she is ready to take the risk, the public interest does not call for a long sentence. Similar reasoning may underlie cases in which an employer's willingness to re-employ a thieving employee procures a lighter sentence. Yet sometimes the situation does not lend itself to any of these interpretations, and the court seems simply to be treating the incident as one in which, however great a nuisance the offender may be, the victim's feelings indicate what is an adequate settlement, although without going to the length of asking the victim exactly what the penalty should be.

In England the Court of Appeal is less often responsive to the victim's forgiveness than sentencers are. In *R. v. Pritchard*[24] it refused to reduce a four-year sentence for his rape of a woman to whom he was related by marriage, in spite of a letter in which she 'begged for mercy and intimated that if she had known that a sentence like this might have resulted she might not have complained'. The Court of Appeal affirmed as its principle that 'the complainant's subsequent attitude relating to the degree of sentence is a completely irrelevant consideration'. In a later case, however,

[24] (1973) 57 Cr. App. Rep. 492ff.

it reduced a three-year sentence on *Parker*[25] for thefts from
the funds of a social club of which he had been secretary.
The decision seems to have been the result of a petition in
his favour by 440 out of about 500 regular members: the
Court said:

> '... We have come to the conclusion that when the
> only part of the local community affected by the
> offence asks for leniency in these terms the Court
> can properly give some effect to their request'.

It did not attempt to reconcile this with its decision in
Pritchard and other cases.

DOUBTFUL CONVICTIONS

In theory, the sentencer must assume that the defendant
has been rightly convicted. He may mitigate sentence for
the sorts of reasons which have been mentioned in this
chapter, but he is not supposed to do so because he himself
believes the defendant to be innocent. Appellate courts may
quash convictions as well as reduce sentences; but unless
they do the former they proceed on the assumption of guilt.
The only place where doubt plays an openly acknowledged
part is in the Home Office and its counterparts in other
countries, when the exercise of the Prerogative of Mercy
('executive clemency' in the U.S.A.) is under consideration.
Not only may pardons be granted without retrials if new
evidence casts serious doubt on the justice of a conviction;
in the days of capital punishment the Home Secretary was
accustomed to commute the death sentence to life imprisonment if he was persuaded that on the evidence available at
the time of the trial there was even a 'scintilla of doubt'
about the guilt of the condemned man. Since juries were

[25] Transcript 122/C/74, which David Thomas very kindly lent me.

not supposed to convict if there was 'reasonable doubt', a scintilla of doubt must have set an even higher standard, which might be described as 'unreasonable but worrying doubt'. Its effect was not to free the accused from any penalty, but to substitute a lesser penalty: an example of mitigation which is hard to justify with strict logic, but not at all hard to understand when the penalty is irreversible. I have not managed, however, to find any non-capital cases in which sentencers have expressly reasoned in this way. All that can be said is that it would be surprising if they had never done so.

Does the opposite ever happen? Defendants are quite often convicted of offences less serious than those with which they were originally charged. Prosecutions for rape may end with convictions for mere indecent assault. Charges of murder often lead to findings of manslaughter. Men indicted for thefts of vehicles frequently persuade courts that the most they can be said to have done was to borrow them without the owners' consent. 'Under-conviction' − to coin a phrase − is paralleled by 'under-charging': every prosecutor is familiar with the sort of case in which he is sure that the defendant was guilty of a more serious offence than that which is indicated by evidence admissible in court. In jurisdictions where plea-bargaining flourishes prosecutors even agree to drop more serious charges which they have a good chance of pressing to a conviction, in exchange for the time and trouble saved by a plea of guilt to a lesser offence.

Do sentencers ever deal more severely with a defendant because they privately believe him guilty of something more serious than his conviction indicates? This is most likely to happen if the court is aware that a guilty plea is the result of a bargain. It is least likely in inquisitorial systems, since these usually require the sentencer himself to determine the category into which the offence falls. In British jury trials it should not in theory happen.[26]

---

[26] See Thomas, pp. 366−70.

I myself, however, have been concerned with two trials in which the charge was murder and the defence was provocation. The contrast between them was interesting. In both the judge indicated strongly to the jury that even if the circumstances had been as the defence claimed they did not indicate sudden provocation of the kind needed to reduce the offence to manslaughter.[27] Both juries however were so sympathetic to the defendant that they decided to accept the defence of provocation. In the English case the judge followed the jury's verdict, though disagreeing with it himself, and sentenced the man to eight years' imprisonment. In the other, Scottish, case the judge disagreed so strongly that he imposed a sentence of 15 years, in effect ensuring that with full remission the middle-aged defendant would be detained for 10 years.[28] Since it was virtually certain that, had he been sentenced to death for murder, his sentence would have been commuted to life, the 15-year sentence ensured that he would remain in prison at least as long as if he had been dealt with as a murderer. Today such a sentence would almost certainly be reduced on appeal.

CONCLUSION

What I have tried to do in this chapter is to show that the many grounds on which sentencers reduce or increase the severity of their penalties imply a variety of justifying aims. Sentencing the offender for the offence, in the sense of matching severity to culpability, is undoubtedly the most common objective; but others are deterrence, the protection of the public, the procurement of co-operation from the offender. Even the strict matching of penalty to culpability is sometimes stretched by taking into account the victim's forgiveness or the offender's moral worth. This last approach is the most questionable, since it assumes a superhuman level

[27] In the Scottish case, 'culpable homicide'.
[28] This was before the introduction of parole.

of insight into the individual. That apart, however, it can be asked whether there is anything wrong with an eclectic approach to the variation of penalties: an approach, that is, which sometimes uses retributive reasoning, sometimes utilitarian. As I have argued elsewhere in Chapter 2 eclecticism in the justification of penalties is not inherently illogical, although it can take illogical forms. A respectable eclecticism must choose in accordance with reasons and rules, not mere reactions; and at present there is no sign that anybody has worked out a reasoned eclecticism. There is in any case one important danger in the eclectic approach: it increases the likelihood of departures from the norm which are, *prima facie* at least, inconsistent. Not only may two sentencers approach similar cases from different standpoints: an eclectic sentencer may apply reductive reasoning to Case A but retributive reasoning to Case B because of some special feature. Even if he is following some rational rule in differentiating, the result may well be a disparity in his sentences which offends people's conception of equity.

Eclecticism must in any case be distinguished from another sort of policy: one which allows departures from normal penalties for reasons unrelated to penal aims of the kind to which a respectable eclectic would appeal. Examples are leniency based on favouritism or bribery, and severity prompted by political motives or racial antagonism. In case these examples suggest, however, that any such departure must be disreputable, let me add 'expediency'. It may be in the interests of Anglo-Soviet relations to deal lightly with a shoplifting Russian athlete.[29] Lighter sentences for informers may help to convict more serious offenders. A pardon for a President *may* protect the status of the Presidency.[30]

---

[29] A problem which arose in the case of Nina Ponomarova in the nineteen-fifties.

[30] It is true that the pardon which Ford gave Nixon was not an exercise of the power to sentence; but it was an exercise of the power to interfere with a sentence which is claimed by all heads of states, and exercised in the name of 'mercy' or 'clemency'.

What attitude should we take towards what I call 'expedient interference with penalties', as distinct from leniency or severity that can be justified by reference to penal aims? The answer will depend on whether the penal system is seen as a system that should be insulated from the law enforcement system or indeed the social system in general. The purist may well find grounds for arguing that it should. The argument, however, cannot be based on the rules of the penal system itself. If it were a game, such as chess or poker, it could be pointed out that it would destroy the game if outcomes could on occasion be decided by extraneous considerations such as the nationality of a player. But it is not a game. By that I do not mean merely that its outcomes are more serious than a defeat at chess or a heavy loss at poker: I am making the logical point that whereas a game would cease to be one if its rules could be over-ridden, predictably or unpredictably, by extraneous considerations, this is not true of penal systems. That they can survive occasional, even frequent, interference of this kind has been demonstrated time and again. The reasons for interference may or may not excite disapproval in the society concerned; and disapproval may reach a level at which it forces reform. The main point is, however, that the approved justifications for penalties, whether retributive or reductive, cannot be logically used as conclusive reasons for outlawing expedient interference with them.

Perhaps the most that can be said by way of prescription is that the grounds for interference should always be (i) explicit and (ii) subject to control by the legislature. This does not necessarily mean that the permissible grounds should be spelt out in statutes. It should certainly be possible for the legislature (i) to criticise a particular instance of expedient interference; (ii) to demand an investigation of it (preferably before rather than after criticising it); (iii) to nullify the interference; and (iv) to legislate against future interferences of a similar kind. To seek, however, to legislate for all conceivable interferences would not only be contrary to the established practice governing the prerogative of heads of states in this area; it would be a virtually impossible task for the draftsmen, and — what is more important — would probably lead to the sort of inflexibility which was attributed to the laws of the Medes and Persians.

7 Stigmatising

The stigmatic effects of being found guilty and sentenced by a criminal court are a well-worn theme of penal reformers and sociologists. There seem to be seven distinguishable kinds:

1. *Suspicion* The offender may become more likely to be suspected of subsequent offences, especially those resembling his original offence. Sometimes the suspicion rests merely on the reputation and increased visibility which he has acquired; but sometimes it is based on his finger-prints or *modus operandi.*

2. *Employment* He may find it harder to get or keep a legitimate job, either because of employers' policies or because of the attitudes towards him which he observes, or thinks he observes, in employers and workmates.

3. *Ostracism* He may lose friends or even his family's support, because of their attitudes or fancied attitudes to him. This may cause him to seek the company of people who are more tolerant of his offence, and who may encourage him in further law-breaking.

4. *Damaged self-image* He may feel 'labelled' as a thief, a drunkard, a man of violence, and may come to regard himself not merely as someone who has once stolen, or got drunk, behaved violently or destructively, but as someone who is 'by nature' likely to do so. If he accepts the label to this extent, and if he is tempted to behave likewise again, he is less likely to regard such behaviour as inconsistent with his nature, and therefore more likely to succumb. He may even feel so degraded that he has nothing to lose by further law-breaking.

5. *Anti-label reaction* On the other hand, he may reject the label as unfair, and be determined to prove to himself or to others that it is. He may behave more rather than less correctly.

6. *Anti-labeller reaction* He may react against the 'labellers' (real or fancied) rather than the label, and reject the values of a society which seems to him unfair, or excessively censorious. He may devote himself to exposing the vices of the Establishment.

7. *Martyrdom* In some special situations his conviction and sentence may appear to some people a great moral wrong, and may enlist support for him or for a cause.

It is assumed by sociologists of 'labelling' that most of these effects are widespread and lasting (the exceptions are 5, 6 and 7, which tend to be ignored). In fact the evidence is scrappy and equivocal. For example, studies which show that prosecuted juvenile delinquents are more likely to commit further delinquencies than unprosecuted delinquents *can* be interpreted in support of 3 or 4; but can also be explained by the supposition that many of the prosecuted delinquents have realised how mild were the consequences of prosecution in their cases. There have been studies and experiments which support 2, at least where white-collar jobs are concerned; but there are also many occupations in which neither employers nor staff ask awkward questions about employees' pasts. As for 5, 6 and 7, they have not been the subject of systematic study. We do not yet have a sociology of martyrdom.

In fact, the assumption that stigma is an automatic and harmful consequence of conviction is to a considerable extent a legacy of an earlier era in which penal systems were deliberately designed to ensure that this was so. The notion that the penalty for breaking the law should be limited to death, deportation, imprisonment, whipping, fining or similar penalties is a modern one. Many nineteenth-century codes either ordained or allowed other formal consequences. Some of these were 'degrading' (to use the French term); conviction of a serious crime entailed loss of what would now be called 'rights',[1] such as voting in constitutional elections, married status, the management of property, the holding of ecclesiastical or political office. Some were precautionary: for example, subjection to police surveillance, or prohibitions on returning to the places where the crimes had been committed.[2]

Some measures — 'peines infamantes' — were deliberately designed to advertise the fact that a person had been found guilty of a crime. An example is branding and other visible mutilations, although in England the practice was eventually reduced to a not very visible burn-mark on the thumb which enabled courts to distinguish 'first offenders' from already convicted felons. The pillory, too, was essentially stigmatising, although it also exposed the offender to other dangers. Formal publication of a conviction for serious crime was part of the French penal code until recently. Nowadays, however, it is not easy to point to a measure which is deliberately stigmatising.

JUDICIAL HOMILIES

It is only in special cases, however, that courts are *prevented* from doing or saying things that are intended or at least bound to affect offenders' reputations: these special cases will be considered later. Otherwise, the considerable discretion which modern sentencers have makes it possible for them to stigmatise in varous ways. In 1978, for example, a judge in Mason County, U.S.A., ordered a marihuana-grower to wheel his plant twenty times round the courthouse in a wheel-barrow for four consecutive Sundays, carrying a notice proclaiming his belief in the legalisation of marihuana use.[3] English courts, while not free to improvise to this extent,

---

[1] The nature of rights is discussed in Chapter 8.

[2] For a review of such measures in European and North American codes, see M. R. Damaska (1968).

[3] *Sunday Times*, 14 April 1978.

often address homilies to the offender. The more censorious these are the more likely they are to be reported by the newspapers. To some extent they are a by-product of the modern expectation that judges should give reasoned justifications for their sentences. A public denigration seems more or less obligatory when an offender appears to the judge to need a severe sentence:

'...You stand utterly disgraced as a husband and a father ...'[4] (R. v. Morgan);

'...I think probably your part in this was more substantial than the two counts to which you pleaded guilty...'[4] R. v. Webster, Longley & Longley);

'...She is a disgrace. She goes out drinking with her boy friend and has more drink than she should and leaves her baby with a baby sitter at home...'[5] (a stipendiary magistrate, sentencing a woman for offences connected with a sports car).

It is not always the defendant, however, who is stigmatised in this way. I was present at Oxford Assizes some years ago when a judge was sentencing a young man who had pleaded guilty to carnal knowledge of a girl not much under the age of 16. Giving him an absolute discharge, he said that he regarded him as blameless, but that the girl's parents were the real culprits. They had of course no way of challenging this statement. More recently, a High Court judge publicly stigmatised a woman who was not on trial. One of her lovers had attacked a former lover with whom she had resumed relations. The judge is reported[6] as having said 'It is a pity we can't have her in the dock. She was the cause of all this... She is a woman of enormous sexual attraction. She was enjoying this situation...'.

[4] I am indebted for these quotations to J. P. Spreutel's unpublished thesis for the Cambridge Diploma in Legal Studies: *Reasons given for Criminal Sentences* (1977) Ch. IV.

[5] *Daily Telegraph*, 30 December 1978.

[6] *Daily Telegraph*, 9 June 1978.

THE STIGMA OF CONVICTION

Whatever the aim of the penalty or the homily, a conviction usually carries some degree of stigma. This can be measured in a rough and ready way by the well known experimental method of sending fictitious written applications for jobs, in which some of the fictitious applicants admit convictions for, say, theft, while others do not. In two experiments of this kind, one in the Netherlands, one in New Zealand, applications which admitted convictions for theft received significantly fewer favourable responses from firms (W. Buikhuisen and F. P. H. Dijksterhuis, 1971; R. Boshier and D. Johnson, 1974).

If of course the offence is not of an unpopular kind, a mere conviction has no such effect. In the experiments just mentioned, some of the applicants admitted convictions not for theft but for drunken driving. In the Netherlands this had almost as adverse an effect as convictions for theft; but in New Zealand the effect was virtually non-existent.[7]

The offence may even be popular. In England, where 'football hooliganism' has aroused a great deal of public disapproval, a policeman who struck a provocative fan in a queue was fined, but received hundreds of sympathetic letters, together with contributions which would have paid for his fine many times over (if they had not been paid to a police charity).[8]

Even if the offence is unpopular, the offender may be immune to its unpopularity, either because he no longer has any close relationships with family or friends, or because his family and friends do not share the values of the majority. Martin and Webster found this to be the case with many of their sample:

[7] It is of course possible that the difference was due to differences in the requirements of the advertised jobs in the two countries: but this seems unlikely.

[8] *Daily Telegraph*, February 1978.

'One has only to recall the high proportion of our men who were living at a rather low level of life, working casually or not at all ... to realize that for many stigma was at most a minor difficulty compared with the problem of getting a living at all. Finally, there were those, about 60 per cent. of our prisoners, who moved in criminal circles where other standards prevail' (1971).

EXPUNGING CONVICTIONS

Nevertheless it is generally assumed that efforts should be made to reduce the stigmatisation of a conviction. Hermann Mannheim says that the idea of effacing *la tache du crime* was first conceived in 17th century France. Like many French penal notions it was theoretical rather than practically effective, for it involved little more than a declaration by the court. It is true that it often meant the restoration of status and rights, although for obvious reasons a marriage which had become void was not reinstated. But for less obvious reasons forfeited decorations or offices were not restored; and nothing was done — apart from the declaration — to efface the memory of the conviction from the minds of the public.

Nowadays many countries have laws which are intended to limit the periods for which a conviction can be officially remembered, as it were.[9] Juveniles apart, these laws fall into two groups: those whose provisions operate automatically, and those in which the convicted person has to apply for their benefit, which the court has discretion to grant or withhold. A good example of the former is Germany, where access to criminal records is restricted after 5 years for minor offences and 10 years for serious ones. Restriction means that the police will not mention the conviction in certificates of good conduct (which are important for getting

[9] For a brief review of such systems see the Gardiner Report (1972).

jobs). Moreover, after 10 years the entry is cancelled, so that the offender can deny having been convicted, *even in court.*

Examples of the discretionary approach can be found in Canada and most of the United States, which use the device of 'pardon' for the purpose. The effect of a pardon of this kind[10] is to restore the offender's civil rights, or in some cases those rights specified in the pardon. It does not cancel the conviction,[11] but is intended as evidence of good subsequent behaviour, and many jurisdictions — Canada again being an example — severely restrict the circumstances in which it is legitimate to refer to the conviction.

Such pardons have to be applied for by the offender, and are granted only when some time has elapsed (2 or 5 years in Canada, depending on the nature of the offence). More important, there is usually an investigation of the offender's recent behaviour; and one awkward feature of the procedure is the way in which this can apprise employers and others of a conviction which was hitherto unknown to them.

Very careful drafting is needed if legislation of this kind is to be effective. In the U.S.A. some States have legislation under which the record of a first conviction is 'expunged': i.e., the record is sealed and the conviction deemed not to have happened. But it is still legitimate to ask if the offender has ever been *arrested*, and if so for what.

A very odd device is the British Rehabilitation of Offenders Act 1974. This was the result of the report of an unofficial committee set up under Lord Gardiner's chairmanship by Justice, the Howard League and NACRO, although the

---

[10] It is also, of course, used, as in most countries, to deal with cases in which real injustice seems to have been done; but here I am concerned only with the special use of it to reduce the disabilities resulting from *just* convictions.

[11] In Canada it 'vacates' it; but this does not apparently entitle the pardoned person to deny the conviction. I am indebted for some of this information to an unpublished LL.M. thesis by Paul Nadin-Davis (1979) *Erasing the Mark of Cain* (in University of Dalhousie Library, Nova Scotia).

final version of the statute differed in many details from the
committee's recommendations. It applies only to convictions
resulting in not more than 30 months' imprisonment. After
a certain period, varying from 6 months to 10 years according to the sentence, the conviction becomes 'spent' and the
offender becomes 'rehabilitated', unless during that period he
receives a non-spendable sentence. A rehabilitated offender
must be treated for all purposes in law as if he had not committed, been charged with, prosecuted for, convicted of,
or sentenced for the offence in question, so that he can safely
deny this, and sue for defamation if it is alleged in a defama-
tory way. There are exceptions, however. He must tell the
truth in certain types of court proceedings, including criminal
proceedings. He must disclose even a spent conviction, if
asked, when applying for certain types of job, e.g., as a
doctor.

The British Act therefore follows the Continental pattern
in operating automatically, but is much more grudging in
various ways. It excludes from its protection some 2,000
offenders a year who receive prison sentences of more than
30 months. It is true that the rest will eventually receive a
fairly comprehensive protection against future mention of
their offence or trial or sentence. But anyone sentenced to
prison will have to wait 7 years, and 10 years if he gets more
than 6 months. If he is fined, he must wait 5 years, but if he
is put on probation or conditionally discharged, only a year
or the period of probation etc., if that is more than a year.
If he is absolutely discharged, he waits 6 months.

This wide variation in waiting periods is, so far as I can
discover, peculiar to the British scheme. The reasoning
which led to it is peculiar in both senses. The Gardiner Committee said 'Clearly, the more serious the offence the longer
it will be before one can be reasonably sure that the offender
has reformed'. Put like this, the argument rests on no empirical evidence. If anything, it is counter to the evidence. One
fairly well-established finding is that crimes of serious personal violence or sexual molestation are the least likely to be

repeated (with the possible exception of violence by terrorists or professional robbers). It is the trivial offences, such
as drunkenness, indecent exposure, soliciting, pilfering which
are the most repetitive. What the Gardiner Committee could
more safely have said is 'The more serious the offence the
more serious for other people will be the *consequences of
mistakenly assuming* that the offender will not repeat it'. But
that would have been relevant only if they were thinking of
the protection of others; and in any case it would have been
a fairly weak argument: the reason, perhaps, why they did
not use it. Again, they could have argued that graver offences
deserve a longer waiting period; but that is a retributive argument which would have been alien to their approach. The
alternative argument which they did offer was that to treat
all offenders alike as regards waiting time would be 'too
radical to command general support'. In other words, they
had a real, political reason, and a pseudo-scientific pretext.

JUVENILE 'CONVICTIONS'

What I have been discussing so far are attempts to wipe out
the effects of conviction *after a period.* But in the case of
juveniles efforts are made to go a stage further and prevent
news of their conviction from being linked with their names
even at the time of conviction. In Britain – and most other
Continental and North American jurisdictions – the public
is excluded from juvenile courts,[12] and the news media
are forbidden to publish particulars which would identify
the juvenile (although in Britain they can report that, say,
a 13-year-old boy was found guilty of malicious damage to
a school, so long as they do not give names and addresses).
In Britain, too, the finding of guilt must be referred to as
such, and not as a conviction.

In many jurisdictions, however, there is a curious anomaly.

[12] Or their equivalent: e.g., 'Children's Hearings' in Scotland.

The ban on identification does not apply if the child is tried
by a higher court, although such trials involve the most stigmatising offences of all – usually homicide. In Britain a
court *may* direct that no identifying particulars be published
about persons under 17 who are concerned in 'any proceedings'.[13] But it often does not. The result is that the careers
of children such as Mary Bell (who at the age of 11 was convicted of killing two small boys in 1968) have been followed
over a period of 10 years by newspapers. It is possible that
in some cases of this kind the judge overlooks his power to
prohibit identification: but there have been cases in which
the defence has asked the judge to exercise it only to have
the request rejected. In one such case,[14] involving an elderly
man who had committed acts of indencency with two young
girls, the judge said that they deserved to be identified. (It is
probably no coincidence that he was the same judge who in
the case mentioned earlier regretted that the woman of
enormous sexual attraction was not in the dock as well as
her lover. In both cases persons who were not accused were
deliberately stigmatised.)

It is arguable, of course, that adults deserve just as much
protection from stigma as juveniles: perhaps more. If one of
the more probable results of a known conviction is to make
it harder to find employment, then it is a more serious matter
for a person of employable age. In Sweden the news media
almost always refrain from identifying adult offenders, even
when they report their trial and conviction. They are under
no statutory prohibition, and they occasionally publish the
name of a notorious offender, such as a member of the
Baader-Meinhof gang who appeared in a Swedish court. But
crime is regarded as bad news rather than interesting gossip,
and privacy is respected, though with curious exceptions
such as peoples' salaries.

[13] S.39 of the Children and Young Persons Act 1933. This was originally limited to proceedings involving indecency or immorality, but this
limitation was removed in the Children and Young Persons Act 1963.
[14] *Daily Telegraph*, June 1978.

Contrast the Swedish press in this respect with the British press. Even a request by a court not to identify a defendant is often disregarded, unless backed up by the law. A good example is this cutting from an English local newspaper in 1978.

In West Germany, the law of privacy ('Personlichkreitsrecht') is regarded as protecting the accused against being photographed or named in news media reports of court proceedings unless there is an over-riding public interest in naming him or her.[15] This exception means that if by reason of his profession (e.g., politician) or behaviour or some notable event he becomes a part of what is called 'contemporary history' he can be named. Otherwise he can sue. Even when a murderer has been publicly identified at his trial and conviction, it was held by the Federal Constitutional Court that when he was about to be released, four years later, a television programme had no right to publish his name and photograph: reporting at a later time was wrong if it would harm the offender.[16]

Student stole after relative's death

A student who shop-lifted after the death of her grandmother was given an absolute discharge by Cambridge magistrates yesterday.

Anne — (25), who gave her address as — Avenue, Cambridge, pleaded guilty to stealing a packet of pears and three grapefruit worth 72p from Bishops Discount.

At the time of the offence she had more than £30 on her, said Mr Michael Pratt, prosecuting.

Miss — , who broke down in court, said her grandmother had died the day before the offence.

The magistrates asked that Miss —'s name and address should not be published, but they made no order.

---

[15] For example, a person or body convicted of libelling another person is required to publish, over their own name, the judgment which exonerates the libelled person. Firms which breach anti-cartel laws, however, can be publicly named.

[16] BVerfG.v. 5 Juni. 1973 BVerfGe Bd. 35, 202ff.

THE ACQUITTED

When conviction is stigmatising, even an acquittal may have a similar, if not quite so strong, effect. In the original experiment in the U.S.A. in which the job-application technique was used (R. D. Schwartz and J. H. Skolnick, 1962)

A. 25 dossiers showed a conviction and sentence for assault;
B. 25 showed an acquittal on a charge of assault;
C. 25 showed a similar acquittal, plus a judge's letter certifying the finding of 'not guilty' and emphasising the legal presumption of innocence;
D. 25 made no mention of any criminal proceedings.

Each dossier was shown to a different employer, whose response was counted as positive if he expressed a willingness to consider the applicant. The numbers of positive responses for each group of 25 were

A. 1
B. 3
C. 6
D. 9

Only one employer was prepared to consider a man convicted of assault. But only three were prepared to consider those who had been acquitted; and even the judge's letter did not seem to make a great difference. It is understandable that employers, given the choice, should prefer men whose records made no mention of a charge of assault to those who had been charged but acquitted. Everyone knows that an acquittal may result from a technicality, a generous jury or a reasonable doubt. At the same time, justice seems to dictate that the acquitted man should be treated as if he had not been tried.

Yet even lawyers have argued differently. In 1975, as a result of a report by the New Zealand Criminal Law Reform Committee, an Act was passed prohibiting the publication of the name of the accused or of any particulars likely to identify him until he was found guilty of the offence and a conviction had been entered by the court.[17] It allowed three exceptions:

1. cases in which the accused himself applied for an order permitting publication of his name; in such cases the court was bound to make such an order;
2. the court could permit publication upon its own motion, upon a prosecutor's application or on the application of a member of the public who considered himself prejudiced by non-publication. Before doing so the court had to consider the nature of the charge, any special circumstances of the case, the possibility of further evidence being offered as a result of publication, the stage which proceedings had reached, and any other relevant matters;
3. if the accused escaped from custody before conviction his name could be published.

This legislation was strongly opposed, chiefly by lawyers and newspapers, on a variety of grounds:

1. nobody could find any similar legislation elsewhere. (But someone has to be the first to take an enlightened step);
2. justice should be seen to be done. (But the Act did not exclude the public from the trial);
3. if the accused were not identified other people could suffer from suspicion. (The examples given were rather unusual);
4. it was illogical to prohibit identification before conviction but not before an appeal against conviction. (What this argument suggests is that the legislation should have gone even further);
5. publishing the name of the accused can lead to further evidence being produced which might assist either the accused or the prosecution, but in either case would reduce the risk of a miscarriage of justice. (So far as the accused was concerned this point had been met

[17] See M. Stace (1976).

by allowing him to demand publication of his name.
So far as the prosecution was concerned, it had to
some extent been met by allowing the Court to permit
publication 'having regard to special circumstances [or]
the interests of the general public ...');
  6. without names trials would not make interesting news.
The last of these reasons is at least honest, although it hardly
amounts to a moral justification. And it does draw attention
to a point to which I shall return later.

The most interesting argument, however, was that put
forward by the New Zealand Law Society:[18]
  7. Acquittal does not necessarily mean innocence. The
     requirement of proof beyond reasonable doubt sets
     a much higher standard than that set for business and
     social purposes.
This implies that for business and social purposes there is no
good reason to distinguish between almost certain guilt and
the mere possibility of guilt. This may well be an accurate
reflection of the way in which the business and social community react; but that does not make it a justification. To
do so, one would have to go further, and argue that only
those who are to some extent morally to blame are prosecuted; but the New Zealand Law Society either did not see
this or realised that it would be going too far.

However that may be, and in spite of the weakness of the
counter-arguments, opposition to the measure, together
with a change of Government, led to its repeal within a
couple of years.

England's only legislative effort to protect the accused
before conviction is confined to rape, and came to pass
almost accidentally. In 1975, the decision of the House of
Lords in *DPP v. Morgan* drew attention to the fact that in
English law if a man has intercourse with a woman in the
genuine belief that she consents he is not raping her, no
matter whether a reasonable man would have known that

---

[18] Which also put forward arguments 2, 3, 4 and 5.

she was not consenting. This scandalised many members of
the public, and especially those who were concerned about
the way in which women were treated by police and defence
lawyers in rape cases. The Heilbron Committee was set up to
review the law of rape, and among the other aspects of the
law on which it invited views from organisations was the possibility of ensuring that the complainant would be anony-
mous. Some of the replies also mentioned the injustice that
could be done to a man who was unjustly accused of rape.
The Heilbron Committee recommended a statutory ban on
the publication of particulars that would identify the complainant (the judge to have power to waive the ban if this
seemed in the interests of justice) but rejected anonymity for
the defendant. They did so on the grounds that he should be
in the same position not as the victim but as other defendants. In any case, they said, 'acquittal will give him public
vindication': an arm-chair assumption which was very different from that of the New Zealand Law Society. Nevertheless, when a Private Member's Bill was introduced to give
effect to most of the Heilbron recommendations, some
Conservative MPs succeeded in carrying an amendment
giving the defendant anonymity until convicted, and this
became law.[19] The result is that if a defendant is charged
with rape his anonymity is protected unless or until he is
convicted; but not if he is charged with indecent assault,
sodomy or any other sexual or non-sexual offence.

ASTIGMATISING OFFENCES

One other approach must be mentioned. There have been
attempts to reduce the stigma of prosecution or conviction
by drawing a distinction between offences which are inevitably regarded as 'criminal' and offences which need
not be. Inevitably, some kinds of offence incur less moral

[19] For a fuller account, see G. Geis (1978).

condemnation than others. Traffic offences are the most obvious example, perhaps because they tend to be regarded as offences of inadvertence or at worst recklessness rather than intentional actions. The way in which law enforcement systems deal with most traffic offences encourages this attitude. Some are disposed of administratively: for example by the 'fixed penalty' (i.e., a 'ticket') in Britain. Even when the offender is prosecuted he is often allowed to plead guilty by post. When asked about an offender's previous convictions, English police usually ignore motoring offences unless the current offence belongs to this category. Even people convicted of serious offences, such as drunk or dangerous driving, seem to find that the effect on their social relationships is minimal. Willett (1964)[20] was told by one dangerous driver that

> 'I found it was like joining a sort of club. One only had to mention the affair in any group and others immediately spoke of their own experiences, rather as people talk about their illnesses ...'.

Another told him that

> 'As usual, from the working class you get nothing but sympathy, and they know how things are; it's the other bastards who point and hint ...'.

It has even been suggested that driving offences should be removed from the jurisdiction of criminal courts, and given to tribunals of another kind. Fitzgerald (1962) suggests 'panels' of 'motoring experts, possibly under the supervision of the motoring organisations'.[21]

More recently it has been argued that petty shoplifting

[20] *Criminal on the Road*, Tavistock, London. See also his later *Drivers after Sentence* (1975, Heinemann, London) for similar findings.

[21] *Criminal Law and Punishment*, Clarendon Press, Oxford. Nevertheless, he believes that 'a really negligent driver is a greater menace ... than a murderer'. His argument seems to be that if we cannot persuade the public to look on such behaviour as immoral, so that the idea of punishing it will be acceptable, 'we may have to abandon the attempt to treat [it] as criminal ...'.

should be taken wholly or partly out of the scope of the criminal law. West Germany has seriously considered a proposal that customers who steal goods of less than a certain value should at most be defendants in civil actions brought by the shops, although in the end legislation took a different form. In England, a group of magistrates (Robert Adley et al., 1979) has argued that, although the law intends that only intentional theft from shops should be a criminal offence, it is so difficult to establish the defence of inadvertence in summary courts that a sharp distinction should be drawn. As at present there should be the offence of deliberate stealing; but as an alternative there should be the possibility of a 'complaint' that a person has taken goods from a shop 'without authority and without making payment'. The latter would be a civil complaint, leading merely to a finding of 'complaint proved' and an order for the return of the goods and 'costs'. Whatever the merits or demerits[22] of this idea, what underlies it is the hope of lessening the stigma in the case of the inadvertent shoplifter.

DIVERSION

One of the strongest arguments for what is called 'diversion' is the avoidance of stigma. Diversion takes several forms. The prosecuting authority may decide not to prosecute, so that the case never appears in court. In England a 'police caution' is in effect a decision of this sort, usually taken before the offender is formally charged. The caution is in effect an irrevocable assurance that the offender will not be prosecuted for the offence in question; and in the case of an adult the caution will not even be mentioned as part of his or her

[22] It would, for example, bring to court some cases of inadvertent removal of goods of the sort which at present are settled on the spot; and to this extent it would *widen* the scope of the law. On the other hand, it might well reduce the number of people who are charged with *theft*.

record in the event of a later appearance in court. In some other jurisdictions, especially in the U.S.A., the prosecutor may have to ask the court for permission not to proceed with the case: if so, publicity is not altogether avoided, although the stigma of conviction is. Sometimes diversion is conditional on the offender's submitting to treatment, or taking part in a scheme of rehabilitation, in which case his offence becomes known to a limited number of people.

THE QUESTIONABLE ASSUMPTION

As I said at the beginning of this chapter, the assumption which underlies nearly all the expedients which have been discussed is that stigma is so harmful that efforts should be made to prevent or limit it so far as this is compatible with justice and the other aims of law enforcement. As I also hinted, it is possible to exaggerate the extent to which offenders are stigmatised, and the ill effects of this. We have so little sound evidence that the subject cries out for systematic study. Yet even if it is assumed that people often or usually suffer to some extent from being labelled as offenders of one sort or another, this does not automatically point to a policy of minimising stigma.

REDUCTIVE ASPECTS

For even if the worst fears of the labelling theorists are true, and stigma increases the likelihood of re-offending, it is possible that the effect of it is a *net* reduction of the total frequency of similar offences. This might come about in one or more of the following ways:

1. It might put potential victims on their guard against identified individuals, as branding used to do, though more efficiently. If this argument is unpopular, it is worth reflecting that Britain 'brands' learner-drivers with L-plates

in order to warn others of the risk which they represent, although they have not been convicted of any motoring offence. It seems paradoxical to tolerate this, while not requiring people who have been convicted of drunk, careless or dangerous driving to carry any sort of visible warning on their vehicles.

2. Where the probable penalty is not severe, the stigma of a court appearance seems to be a more powerful deterrent.

There is some empirical evidence to support this. Willcock and Stokes found that English males in their late 'teens ranked the 'publicity or shame' of a court appearance higher in their list of deterrents than the likely punishment (1963). An example of the deliberate use of this deterrent was ' The John Hour" on New York's municipally-owned radio and television stations. This was part of the Mayor's campaign to reduce street soliciting by prostitutes, and involved broadcasting the names of men convicted of resorting to prostitutes.

3. The public punishment of offenders may promote a society's moral cohesiveness. This has been argued by Durkheimian sociologists. If it is true (and it may not be true in the case of conduct about which a society is in two or more minds, such as pornography) then it is arguable that this effect is likely to be enhanced by stigmatising as well as punishing offenders, provided at least that the stigmatic effects are not so obviously inhumane as to excite sympathy for them. Admittedly, like so many generalisations of early sociologists, this is really arm-chair psychology, empirically untested. What is more, even if it is the case that public punishment for an offence increases a community's moral cohesion, how much extra cohesion is achieved by identifying the culprit? It may be the case that the naming of a friend, an acquaintance or a public figure dramatises the punishment in an effective way; but this is less likely if the identified person is a nobody.

Unfortunately, what is almost certain is that if news media could not identify defendants they would report far fewer trials. On the whole, therefore, if you are a thorough-going utilitarian who believes that the reduction of shop-lifting, rape, *etc.*, is for the general good, if you also believe that stigma prevents more instances of these than it produces, and if you have no retributive or humanitarian reservations, you must logically favour the maximising of stigma.

But those reservations are important. If you are merely the sort of retributivist who holds that only the undoubtedly guilty should be penalised, but does not believe that the form or severity of penalties should be commensurate with or pro-portional to culpability, then you need not be disturbed by a policy of maximising stigma in the interests of crime-reduction. You should of course be deeply disturbed by the attitude of the New Zealand Law Society, who argued, as I have said, that there should be no ban on identifying *acquitted* people because for business and social purposes we do not insist on being sure beyond reasonable doubt. But where convicted offenders are concerned you need not be worried.

It is the punisher − the retributivist who believes in com-mensurate or proportional punishment − who has to worry about stigma, and not only about deliberate stigmatising but also about non-prevention of stigma. For it can be argued that, if the punishment ordered by the court is meant to be commensurate or proportional to the offence, any extra hardship resulting from stigma will distort the balance between the offence and the punishment. To which the retributivist can only reply that the stigma is not ordered by the court, and is not part of the punishment. Even some punishers, however, would regard this as a specious argument, and would comment that the sentencer should take into account what he knows to be the inevitable consequences of conviction and punishment for the offender, just as it is arguable that he should take into account the effect of a custodial sentence on a man's job or a housewife's home. It is a 'natural punishment' (see p.130), even if it is a conse-quence of the conviction rather than the crime. The senten-cer could reply that the hardship of stigma is much harder to estimate than the hardship of a fine or imprisonment, and

varies so much according to the offender's situation and
future behaviour that it cannot be made part of a calcula-
tion, or at best must be assumed to be equal for all offenders.
But this is obviously unrealistic. A person's first conviction
for dishonesty does much more damage to his reputation
than does a second or a third. People whose success in their
occupation depends on the assumption that they are honest
will suffer more harm than employees of other kinds.

The punisher seems to have three choices. He can stick to
the pure but artificial argument that all the sentencer is
concerned with is making sure that the official punishment
is appropriate to the offender's culpability. If so, he must
be careful to apply the same principle to the consideration of
other pleas in mitigation, and disregard any which are based
on the argument that the offender will suffer in any case as
a result of his offence or his conviction.[23]

Alternatively, the punisher may attempt the very difficult
task of taking stigma (and other consequences) into account.
If he attempts this, he must think about mitigation and
aggravation with much more sophistication than English or
American judges have been used to.

His third course is to decide that retributive justice requires us to confine the effects of sentences to the official
penalty, so far as this can be done. This involves trying to
minimise stigma, even if this means reducing the deterrent
efficacy of the law enforcement system.

A policy of minimising stigma would involve:

1. prohibiting the public identification of offenders not
   only before conviction but also after it;
2. extending the protection afforded by the Rehabilitation
   of Offenders Act so that it applied irrespective of the
   sentence;
3. prohibiting the public disclosure in court of previous
   convictions, even when they are taken into consideration at the sentencing stage.

[23] Of course not all pleas in mitigation are of this kind, as Chapter
6 makes plain.

SUMMARY

The purpose of this chapter, however, is not to argue the case for minimising stigma: only the case for working out a consistent and tenable policy. To sum up:

1. Most of the 'labelling' effects of conviction and sentence are, if and when they occur, harmful to the individual defendant.
2. We ought therefore to consider very carefully to what extent, and how, these effects should be controlled.
3. For example, it seems unjust that judges should be allowed to make comments which stigmatise people who have not been on trial.
4. It also seems unjust to allow news media to identify the accused before he has been found guilty and had a chance to appeal against conviction.
5. As for juveniles, if we protect them against identification in juvenile courts it is inconsistent not to give them the same protection in other courts.
6. But to protect convicted adults against public identification (as the Swedish news media do, for example) would be to surrender a powerful deterrent.
7. Believers in commensurate or proportionate retribution ought to be more concerned than they are either to take stigma into account or to minimise it.
8. This could be done without altogether sacrificing it as a deterrent: for example by prohibiting the identification of 'first offenders'.

8 Righting

'Prisoners' rights' are children of the 'Human Rights' of the European Convention, in turn begotten by the more ambitious − though less forceful[1] − United Nations Declaration of Human Rights. Human Rights are descendants of *The Rights of Man* (the title of Paine's famous pamphlet), and the Bills of Rights of England and Virginia, the American Declaration of Independence, and the political philosophy of John Locke. The concept of individuals' rights, although said to be lacking in Roman Law,[2] has been traced as far back as de Vittoria (1532),[2] William of Occam (the 14th century razor-wielding heretic) and even the pre-Christian Stoic philosophers.[3] As we shall see, the notion is by no means universally accepted, even in the political theories of Western societies; but there can be no doubt that in the second half of this century it has once again become an influential political idea.

[1] 'Less forceful' because unlike the European Convention they are declaratory rather than binding, and no machinery for enforcement is provided. As for the United Nations' Standard Minimum Rules for the Treatment of Prisoners, adopted at the First U.N. Congress on the Prevention of Crime and the Treatment of Offenders in 1955, these do not rely on the concept of rights. There is a reference in Rule 57 to the curtailment of the right of self-determination which is involved in deprivation of liberty; but the Rule implies that this is acceptable. The Rules as a whole borrow extensively from the English Prison Rules of the nineteen-fifties.

[2] See Stein and Shand (1974).

[3] See Cranston (1973), whose short history of 'human rights' is a most informative book.

The parties to the European Convention on Human Rights agreed in 1948 to protect the rights of individuals to

life
liberty
security of person;

and more specifically

freedom from slavery
freedom from torture
freedom from forced labour
freedom of thought, conscience and religion
freedom of expression and assembly
the right to privacy
the right to marry
the right to form trade unions;

with the later additions of

freedom of movement
the right to own property
the right to have one's children educated in accordance with one's religion or philosophy;

but adding the important reservation that most of these rights or freedoms could be subject to such restrictions as are prescribed by law and are necessary in a democratic society for certain specified purposes.

The U.S.A. is not of course a party to the European Convention; but the rights enshrined in the Constitution of 1776 and later amendments have provided American lawyers with even more leverage, exerted through the courts. The American citizen probably enjoys more protection of this kind, at least in legal theory, than the nationals of any other country.

There can be no doubt that the notion of rights, in countries which genuinely accept it, has had a beneficial impact on the quality of life, has reduced indefensible inequalities, and has occasionally sabotaged oppression. One consequence of this, however, is that any attempt at a critique of rights, at a rational discussion of their nature, is apt to be regarded as an illiberal reaction. Nevertheless, the language of rights is now being used so rhetorically, which means with emotion rather than precision, that some corrective is necessary.

PRISONERS' RIGHTS

'Prisoners' rights' exemplifies the rhetorical and unreflective use of the notion. The very fact that the phrase is not 'offenders' rights' emphasises that it is a slogan rather than a term of art. It is true that prisoners can suffer from more inhumane deprivations than offenders who are subjected to non-custodial penalties or treatments. But it is the popular appeal of 'prisoners' rights' rather than anything peculiar to them which has given them the status of a specialty.

The distinction between the rhetorical and the realistic may become clearer if we begin with the fundamental question 'What sort of a thing is a right?'.

NATURAL RIGHTS

Some people believe in rights which are 'natural': that is, a part of nature, independent of man-made laws or rules. Men may come to recognise natural rights and embody them in laws, but they do not thereby create them. Believers in natural rights may or may not also believe in man-made rights. If they do not, they have to find some other name for the obligations conferred by contracts, promises, or statutes which purport to confer rights. But belief in natural rights is usually combined with belief in man-made rights.

Indeed, it is questionable whether there are any natural rights at all, or only man-made ones. Since a right is not something that can be observed, like a wind or a spatial relation or a magnetic field, but only something that can be defined — and even that with varying precision and acceptability — it is impossible to settle this by demonstration. One can easily point to man-made rights, such as rights to welfare payments, to tenancies, to things promised in a contract: they are there to be seen in the statute, the regulations or the contract. But where would one look for a natural right?

'Into the nature of moral codes', would be a philosopher's answer.[4] The notion of a right may turn out to be indispensable to such codes. This would not necessarily be disproved by pointing to codes such as those of Plato or Aristotle which are said to do without the notion: perhaps *modern* morality needs the notion?

It must be pointed out that it is one thing to need the notion of a right, but another thing to need a specified right. The notion of money is essential to banking, but a particular currency is not. It could be that the notion of a right is an indispensable part of modern ideas of morality, but that the specific content, as it were, of rights might vary from one code to another, as currencies do in banking. One might similarly believe that the notion of a promise is indispensable to certain social institutions, such as marriage, without being specific about the content of the promises involved.

In other words, it is possible to regard the concept of a right as essential to modern morality without implying that a particular right — say to freedom of speech — exists independently of man-made laws or rules. In this sense it *is* arguable that since modern morality (and many older codes of conduct) includes the notion of a promise, and since a promise confers on the person to whom a promise is made the right to claim its fulfilment or not, as he chooses, at least this sort of right is 'natural'. All that is really being said of course, is that a promise is by definition something

[4] Some philosophers, however, such as Locke and Nozick, simply treat natural rights as axiomatic, and take for granted that the reader acknowledges their existence.

that confers such a right: one could not have promises without it. If we thought of promises merely as vows from which
people could not be released by the people to whom they
were made, the notion of a promise would not involve a
right, only an unconditional obligation. A right is something
which is claimed or not, at the choice of the person to
whom the right belongs.

It is much harder, however, to point to a right with a
particular content which can be regarded as implied in
the same way by some essential feature of modern moral
codes. Hart has argued (1955) that 'if there are any moral
rights at all, it follows that there is at least one natural right,
the equal right of all men to be free'. His argument is
simple and neat. To assert a right is to assert a moral justification for interference with another's freedom; so that the
notion of a right could have no place in morals unless it is
recognised that such interference requires moral justification.

Two points have to be made, however. Hart's argument
depends, as he expressly says, on there being such things
as moral rights. If there were not, or in a moral code which
did without the notion, his argument would not apply.
Secondly, if and where his argument does hold good, the
right which it shows to be 'natural' − that is, implicit in the
notion of all other moral rights, however generated − is an
unspecific one: the right to choose to exercise whatever other
rights one has. Like the right to claim what has been promised to oneself, this is a fairly formal right, without much
specific content.

LIBERTIES

In making his point, however, Hart draws attention to the
important distinction between 'rights' which have the

obligations of others as correlatives[5] and what he calls 'liberties', following Bentham. The latter do not seem to have correlative *obligations*, and Hart's example is the liberty to choose whether to exercise a moral right (or presumably a legal right). It entails no duty on the part of anyone else to do anything, apart from refraining from interference with the liberty.

IMMUNITIES

Another sub-species of right, to which Hohfeld drew attention, is 'immunities'. In his terminology an immunity was 'freedom from the legal power or control of another as regards some legal relation' (1913). Diplomatic immunity is the exemption of a diplomat from prosecution or other legal proceedings in circumstances which would otherwise justify this. It is almost true to say also that children under the age of criminal liability are immune from a finding of guilt, since whatever the truth may be they are conclusively *presumed* incapable of *mens rea*. These examples apart, however, offenders are hardly ever said to have immunities.

GENERAL RIGHTS

Hart also distinguishes 'general' from 'special' rights. The latter arise out of special relationships (as when children have a right to inherit a parent's property) or transactions (such as promises or contracts). The former 'are rights which all men capable of choice have in the absence of special conditions which give rise to special rights' (1955). He applies the same

[5] A technical term applied by Hohfeld (1913) to the analysis of rights. As Locke said, being a husband implies having a wife. Certain rights imply that someone else has a correlative duty, whether to do something if asked by the person who has the right, or not to do something that would interfere with the exercise of the right.

distinction to liberties; so that he talks of general rights, general liberties, special rights and special liberties. His example of the last of these categories, however, shows how rare and subtle it is:

> 'If you catch me reading your brother's diary, you say 'You have no right to read it'. I say 'I have a right to read it — your brother said I might unless he told me not to, and he has not told me not to'. Here I have been specially licensed by your brother who had a right to require me not to read his diary, so I am exempted from the moral obligation not to read it, but your brother is under no obligation to let me go on reading it ...' (*ibid.*).

But if your brother had not reserved the right to withdraw his permission, this would, apparently, have been a special *right*, not a special liberty.

The generality of Hart's rights and liberties, however, is subject to at least one limitation. They can be attributed only to people who are capable of choice; or, more precisely, capable of choosing whether to claim them or not. As we have seen, a right involves an obligation on the part of someone else, but an obligation from which the possessor of the right can release him. It seems to follow that if the person who is supposed to have the right is incapable of choosing between claiming and not claiming it, he does not really have the right after all. Hart therefore concludes that children and animals cannot have rights. This will take some people aback. The rights of children are so generally accepted that legal systems even provide for the appointment of guardians to see that they are respected and if necessary to claim them. The United Nations agreed in 1966 on a Declaration of the Rights of the Child. As for the rights of animals, UNESCO has recently drafted a charter dealing with these, and some people are now asserting the rights of plants and even the inorganic environment, so powerful is the rhetorical force of the word.

Yet Hart's point cannot be brushed aside. It is no solution to point out that even young children *are* capable of choice – for example between a piece of chocolate and a toffee. That is not the same thing as choosing between separated parents, or choosing between being prosecuted and accepting a caution (or some other form of diversion). Sometimes, of course, skilled advice is all that the child needs to enable him to choose. But a child may be so young that he cannot be got to understand the nature of the choice. In such cases the usual legal approach is to provide for the appointment of someone to exercise the choice on his behalf. But how can the child be said to have a right to exercise if he cannot himself make a proper choice?

One solution is to argue that, while he indeed does not have a right, others have the obligation which is the correlative of the right; but since, if he had been capable of choice, he might have chosen to release them from the obligation, someone else with the child's interests at heart should be empowered to choose. A simpler solution is to argue that defining rights as things which their owners can claim or not, as they choose, does not logically entail denying rights to someone because he is incapable of such a choice. A promise to a child can be fairly said to give the child the right to insist on its fulfilment even if the child is incapable of understanding when it would be in his interests not to insist. This does not necessarily mean that the promiser is always morally bound to keep the promise. There may be justifications for overriding rights; and that is the subject of the following sections.

ABSOLUTE RIGHTS

To conclude that a right is natural or general is not to conclude that it is absolute. An 'absolute' right (or liberty or immunity) is one which cannot ever be curtailed without the commission of a moral wrong. 'Curtailment' is usually taken to mean 'limitation without the consent of the person to whom the right (etc.) belongs'. For just as people are regarded as not obliged to insist on their rights — that is, as free to 'waive' them in particular situations (as with the keeping of promises) — so they are regarded as free to 'surrender' them: that is, to waive a right in a whole category of situations, or in general. Some people would argue that there are rights which are absolute in an even stricter sense, and which they cannot choose to waive or surrender without committing a moral wrong. An example might be the right to life, although it is difficult to sustain the argument when someone chooses to give up his life in order to preserve lives which he values more than his own. It is not easy to find a convincing example of a right which is absolute in this sense.

FORFEITURE

Forfeiture is another matter. In the case of many man-made rights the rules which create them expressly declare that they cease to be rights if the person to whom they are granted fails to fulfil certain conditions. I forfeit my right to welfare payments by failing to make the required financial contributions. Forfeiture may be temporary, as in this case, or permanent. In the nineteenth-century French Penal Code some offenders forfeited rights such as voting and their married status.

Should a man-made right be forfeitable through sheer inadvertence? We are inclined to behave as if we thought not. We think that someone who is in danger of forfeiting his right to welfare payments or insurance benefits through inadvertent failure to keep up his contributions or premiums ought to be warned of this, so that he has the chance to remedy his oversight. Certainly we are happier about forfeitures when they have been incurred as a result of a deliberate choice. This seems to accord with Hart's insistence that a right cannot be attributed to someone who lacks the capacity for choice: the corollary seems to be that it can be surrendered or forfeited only by choice.

OFFENDERS' RIGHTS

This point is especially important when offenders' rights are the issue. Some penal systems — such as the French — lay considerable emphasis on offenders' forfeiture of rights. Others have little or nothing to say on the subject. In England and Scotland the only civic right which is expressly declared forfeit is the right to vote, and that only while an offender is serving a custodial sentence.[6] A court is expressly empowered to disqualify a person convicted of a company fraud from being a company director. There are restrictions for ex-prisoners as regards jury service and firearms' licences; but firearms' licences are so sparingly granted that ordinary citizens find it hard to get one even with a clean record.

It is not these forfeitures however that are the subject of criticism, but those which are imposed by administrative rules, or simply by the way in which custodial establishments are conducted. Until recently a prisoner could not consult a solicitor, let alone initiate legal proceedings, without the permission of the Home Office, which was by no means always given. The Prison Rules were amended as a result of a successful application by Golder to the European Court of Human Rights;[7] and English prisoners can now communicate freely with their solicitors on the subject of litigation, and institute proceedings. On the other hand they still need special permission to be present at court hearings (unless of

[6] 'Felons' used to forfeit land and property (until 1890) and could not serve in the armed forces (in theory), hold office under the Crown, occupy ecclesiastical benefices or be Members of Parliament (until 1967).

[7] European Court of Human Rights; Judgment of 21 February 1975, *Golder v. United Kingdom*, Series A, No. 18.

course they are on trial themselves): the reason seems to be that quite a number of prisoners have made temporary escapes while in or near courts.

Even a prisoner who is not litigious is likely to be embarrassed by the censoring of his incoming and outgoing letters. In the case of a free citizen this would be regarded as a violation of his right to privacy.[8] The censoring of mail in the armed forces is held to be justified as a counter-intelligence measure. In prisons the justifications given are that otherwise some prisoners would threaten witnesses, make allegations which would be unfairly damaging to staff or fellow-inmates (especially if they reached the sensational newspapers), concert plans for escape or smuggle in money or drugs; and certainly when prisoners succeed in evading censorship they sometimes do such things.

Most important of all, perhaps, is the protection of prisoners against physical harm inflicted by other inmates and staff. Even in Britain, where an officer who assaults a prisoner without the excuse of self-defence is liable to prosecution and dismissal, such assaults occur from time to time, as recent trials have confirmed. Much more frequent are assaults by inmates on each other. It is arguable that when it is thought necessary to commit a man or woman to custody in the company of other inmates believed to contain a higher percentage of violent offenders than the ordinary population, those who have charge of them are under an obligation to do what is reasonably practicable to protect them. Certainly English courts have held that prison authorities have 'a common law duty ... to take reasonable care for the safety' of prisoners.[9] The English (and Scottish) Prison Rules not only

[8] This is another example of a 'right' which is generally asserted, but does not always rest on a legal foundation, especially in Britain.

[9] See *Ellis v. Home Office* [1953] 2 All E. R. 149 (C.A.). It is true that, as this and other cases have demonstrated, it is not easy for plaintiffs to convince courts that this reasonable care was not taken: but at least one plaintiff has succeeded in doing so (see *D'Arcy v. Prison Commissioners* (1955); *The Times*, 15–17 November).

allow governors to order the segregation of prisoners for their protection: they also allow prisoners to ask for segregation – a request which is nearly always granted.[10]

It is worth noting, however, that 'reasonable care' is all that the courts demand: not elaborate precautions which would make the prisoner safer inside than outside. The man in the street is always at some risk of being assaulted: a risk which varies from slight to considerable according to the places he frequents, his conduct and other circumstances less within his control. If he is assaulted, the State is not usually regarded as having culpably failed in a duty to provide him with complete protection.[11]

What ought to be made explicit in discussions of such issues are two questions. What was the extent of the right which the prisoner had under the law before imprisonment? Did he forfeit it when sentenced? Conjugal visiting provides a good example. If he was married and not legally separated from his wife, he had a 'conjugal right' to sexual intercourse with her (and she with him); but the correlative of this right was an obligation on the part of his spouse, and not an obligation on the part of anyone else to facilitate intercourse. On the other hand, whether married or not, he can be regarded as having had a 'liberty' to copulate with any consenting adult partner, but nobody had a corresponding obligation to copulate with him. By imprisoning him the court did not repudiate any obligation on the part of the State; what it did was to curtail a liberty.

Was the curtailment justified? Could the liberty be said to have been declared forfeit? The law gives the State the right to keep him in custody for a period; but it does not

[10] Occasionally a governor comes to the conclusion that the prisoner can safely be looked after in the main part of his prison, or that the ostensible reason for the request was not the real one.

[11] During the campaign for State compensation for victims or criminal violence in the early nineteen-sixties it *was* sometimes argued that the State had failed in its duty whenever a citizen was assaulted; but this argument was rejected by the Home Office's Working Party (1961).

say anything about this liberty. Is it implicitly forfeit? Judges who sentence people to imprisonment know that they are thereby depriving them of certain liberties, but do not expressly order this. Some people would argue that if imprisonment is to have any retributive or deterrent value it should entail such deprivations; and that if their propriety is questionable because they are not expressly ordered then they should be expressly ordered. Others would object that it is a deprivation which curtails the rights of innocent spouses. They could argue that it may well be difficult for over-crowded prisons to provide conjugal visits in decent conditions; but that if this particular liberty were expressly declared forfeit prison authorities would feel justified in imposing this deprivation even when conjugal visiting or home leave was both practicable and in the interests of the prisoner's family life.

Can it be claimed that prisoners themselves have implicitly chosen to forfeit such rights or liberties when choosing to commit their offences? Certainly it is arguable that a man who plans a robbery knows that he is risking imprisonment, however high he rates his chances of escaping conviction. Unless he is exceptionally ignorant he knows the deprivations involved in imprisonment. He therefore chooses the risk of forfeiting certain liberties. Two points must be made about this argument. One is that by no means all offenders can be said to 'choose' to commit their offences, in the sense of wondering whether they should or not. Some act impulsively, some compulsively, some more or less habitually. Even if this is conceded, however, the most that it establishes is a case for mitigating the 'pains of imprisonment' — or substituting a lesser penalty — for offenders who did not make a considered choice. It leaves unchallenged the argument that at least some prisoners have knowingly risked the forfeiture of certain rights and liberties.

The important question is whether even the man who premeditates his crime in full knowledge of the conditions of imprisonment can be said to be choosing to risk the forfeiture

of rights and liberties if that forfeiture is not expressly
declared by law to be part of the permissible penalty. Some
people would argue that if this is not so the rights and
liberties have not been forfeited, and ought not therefore to
be infringed unless it is impossible to impose the specified
penalty without doing so.

This seems to be the underlying rationale of the Prisoners'
Bill of Rights promulgated by the American Friends' Service
Committee (1971), which begins:

'Prisoners are entitled to every constitutional right
exercised by the outside population except for those
inherently inconsistent with the operation of the institution. The burden must be on the institution to show
why it is necessary to deprive inmates of certain rights,
rather than on the inmates to show why they should not
be deprived of them.'

It must be recognised, however, that the exception of rights
and liberties 'inherently inconsistent with the operation of
the institution' can be interpreted in a variety of ways, some
of them generous, some oppressive. If the institution is
intended to hold prisoners whose escape would be regarded
as a serious danger, such things as privacy of correspondence,
or unsupervised visits by relatives and friends, could be
regarded as 'inherently inconsistent with the operation' of
the prison.

For example, the first specific right in the Bill is:
'1. Unrestricted access to the courts and to confidential
    legal counsel from an attorney of the individual's
    choosing or from a public defender ...'.
From the point of view of security experience has shown —
for example in the case of the Baader-Meinhof defendants —
that not all lawyers of the individual's choosing can be
trusted not to smuggle in weapons or other means of sub-
verting security. Unrestricted access to courts involves escorts
— and sometimes elaborate policing — which make heavy

demands on manpower. A solution sometimes adopted is to hold the court inside the institution: but this means severe restrictions on the numbers and sorts of people who are allowed to be present at the hearings, which in turn gives rise to suspicions about the fairness of the proceedings.

'Freedom from compulsion to work', another item in the same document, gives rise to more complex problems. Prisons are expensive places to run. In England a medium security prison costs as much per inmate-week as an open mental hospital or the charges of a cheap commercial hotel. These costs would be much higher if it were not for the use of prisoners as cleaners, kitchen staff, librarians, launderers, tailors, shoemakers and so forth. Does this justify compulsion to work? A prison which could not count on its kitchen staff for regular work would soon be the subject of even more criticism than one which compelled them to turn up. Even the European Convention on Human Rights prohibits 'forced labour' only for offenders who are dealt with *non*-custodially.[12]

What is arguable is that prisoners should not be compelled to work in manufacturing industries. In many prison systems which produce goods for sale the so-called profit does no more than cover the cost of equipment, raw materials and technical supervision: the prisons would cost the taxpayer no more – and sometimes a little less – if they made no attempt at industrial production. Should prisoners be compelled to do such work? The argument that it makes them more likely to be good workers after release is now undermined by the evidence. So is the hope of qualifying them for more skilled jobs, at least in countries with high unemployment and strict trades unions. Probably the only

[12] It is sometimes said that Canadian prisoners are under no obligation to work; but this is not the case, at least so far as Federal penitentiaries are concerned. Refusal to work can be treated as a disciplinary offence. What has happened is that the new device of 'earned remission', which takes voluntary work into account, has made it virtually unnecessary to invoke the disciplinary procedure.

justification which stands up to a critical examination is that, for those whose work does not contribute to cheaper maintenance of the prison, compulsory production at least fills their time, and by doing so lessens boredom, and the risk of internecine feuding or organised indiscipline. But an unqualified 'freedom from compulsion to work' would raise problems about which the American Friends' Service Committee are silent.

CURTAILMENT

Some people would grant that rights and liberties can properly be voluntarily waived or surrendered, or forfeited by an informed choice; but would question whether they can be curtailed: that is, restricted or abrogated without the consent of those to whom the rights and liberties are said to belong. It is true that the European Convention on Human Rights includes the reservation that its rights and liberties can be subject to such specified restrictions as are prescribed by law and are necessary in a democratic society. But this reservation was inserted as a concession to signatories who would otherwise have refused to sign. The United States Constitution contains hardly any reservations of this kind: its rights can be waived, perhaps surrendered or forfeited, but not, in theory at least,[13] curtailed.

The historical reason for this is that the American Declaration of Independence was inspired by the political philosophy of Locke, who saw the main purpose of political society as being the protection of man's natural rights to life, freedom and property.[14] Even holders of this view, however, are not bound by it to regard *any* curtailment of natural rights

---

[13] In practice some of them are: the right to carry arms is subject to restrictions on the kind of weapons and the persons who may carry them (parolees for instance).

[14] 'Property' was replaced in the Declaration by 'the pursuit of happiness'!

by the State as unjustified. It may prove impracticable to safeguard the natural rights of members of the society in general without interfering to some extent with the rights of some or all members. If some members own so much of the available food as to threaten the lives of others, the right to life will probably be regarded as over-riding the right to property. If one man's exercise of the right to 'pursue happiness' threatens the lives or happiness of others, something has to give way. Undeniably, however, Locke's political philosophy has been coupled with the view that certain rights are 'imprescriptible'; that is, absolute. The important point is that neither view is logically entailed by the other.

If, on the other hand, you believe that the authority of the State is based on some sort of social contract, then the question whether the State can justifiably curtail the rights of some or all members depends on two things:

(i) whether its members are regarded as having any rights other than those granted by the State, and

(ii) what the contract says about those rights.

In Hobbes' version of the social contract men did have natural rights, but had to give up nearly all of them in order to get good government. Since, however, the social contract is never expressly set out on paper, being really a philosopher's fiction,[15] what the *contract* has to say about the curtailment of rights by the State is anybody's guess. A more sensible question is 'What does the Constitution have to say?' − if you have a written constitution.

Theories which rely on the notion of 'consent to be governed' rather than a social contract do not make it much easier to decide whether the State can curtail rights. In the

---

[15] It is said that there was a literal social contract in the case of the American colonies. But even this can hardly be said to bind the descendants of the original contractors.

first place, the consent is usually[16] no more real than the contract. More important, however, is the point that neither 'social contract' nor 'consent' theories really help us to decide about the propriety of curtailing rights against the will of the subject. For they are both attempts to argue that in some way the subject *has* consented to the modification of any rights he has.

In contrast, theories based on the notion of 'the general will' have no difficulty in justifying curtailment of rights irrespective of the wishes of those to whom the rights are ascribed. It is true that 'the general will' is just as much of a fiction as 'the social contract', and even more ambiguous in meaning. But on almost any interpretation it can override the rights of subjects, whether natural or man-made. The most that can be asked of the general will is that it should observe due process of law. The same can be said of theories which base the State's authority on 'the common good'.[17]

For Idealist philosophers, on the whole, the problem does not arise. If they recognise rights — and some do not — it is the rights of 'the community' or of 'the people'.[18] For Marx, the rights of man were a bourgeois illusion, and only when people ceased to think of themselves as individuals with rights would the human species achieve its potential. This has not prevented Marxist countries, notably the USSR itself, from recognising certain individual rights in their laws; but this seems to be a concession to Western views (long before President Carter's initiative) rather than a genuine modification of the Marxist theory of the State. As Alice Tay (1978) remarks, there is within modern Marxism 'a certain tension over human rights and a certain ambivalence

[16] It *can* be real, however, when someone voluntarily changes nationality; but then he is being forced to choose between forms of government, and not between government and no government.

[17] For an excellent exposition of the different types of theory, see D. D. Raphael's *Problems of Political Philosophy* (1976) Chapter 7.

[18] See F. H. Bradley (1884) and the German Liberals' Declaration of Rights of 1848, cited by Maurice Cranston (1973).

towards them', although as she emphasises this state of affairs is not confined to communist countries or socialist parties.

DISCRIMINATION

This does not, however, dispose of the problem of curtailment. Whatever political theory we hold, or even if we have none, we may be prepared to accept the proposition that the State is justified in curtailing the rights of its members, but at the same time insist that in doing so it should not discriminate between categories, such as slaves and freemen, women and men, blacks and whites, minority and majority religions. Whether a right or a liberty is natural or man-made, we regard it as wrong to interfere with it unless

either (a) its owner has freely consented,

or (b) we have a *moral* (and not merely a practical) justification for interfering with it.

And normally we do not regard slavery, femininity, race or religious belief as a basis of moral justification. Indeed, a principle of 'no discrimination', or 'no discrimination on specified grounds' can be held even by people who do not believe in rights of any kind. Of course it can be translated into a right of sorts: the right not to be discriminated against, or discriminated against on certain grounds. But such a translation is pointless: it adds no justification, and does not provide any more precise guidance in putting the principle into practice.

We should therefore consider whether instead of talking about 'offenders' rights', a phrase which does not help us to decide whether a right is inalienable, or forfeitable, or curtailable, penologists might find it more helpful to talk about 'discrimination against offenders'. One or two codes have approached the problem in this way. The United Nations' Standard Minimum Rules for the Treatment of Prisoners does not rely on the concept of rights, but instead bans 'discrimination on grounds of race, colour, sex, religion, political or other opinion, national or social origin, property, birth or other status' (1955, Rule 1). The Hawaiian Employ- ment Relations Act makes it 'unlawful discrimination to refuse to employ anyone, or to discharge him because of his race, sex, age, religion, colour, ancestry *or arrest and court records which do not have a substantial relationship to the functions and responsibilities of the ... employment'*. The Canadian Human Rights Act declares as a principle that people should not be hindered from making for themselves the lives they wish by 'discriminatory practices based on race, national or ethnic origin, colour, religion, age, sex or marital status, *or conviction for an offence for which a pardon has been granted ... '*.

Admittedly these codes are cautious in scope. The United Nations' Standard Minimum Rules apply only to prisoners. Hawaii's Act deals only with employment; Canada's only with offences for which pardons have been granted (see p.148). Moreover, 'discrimination', once a neutral word, now has its own rhetorical aura, so that a rule or practice which deals differently with different categories of people can be condemned by simply saying 'But that's discrimina- tion'.

It is worth considering for a moment the innumerable ways in which we do make distinctions by rule or practice which are not condemned as discriminatory. For example:

(a) children are distinguished from adults in many ways, usually for their own protection. Below a certain age one is not free to smoke, drink alcohol, have sexual intercourse, enter into contracts;

(b) persons without certain qualifications are prohibited from giving certain kinds of medical treatment;

(c) certain premises, such as clubs, can be used only by people who have paid for the privilege, or been accor- ded it by already privileged people;

(d) people are not allowed to drive certain kinds of vehicle, or fly aircraft, without evidence of their skill in doing so;

(e) people are not accepted for certain kinds of training or education unless they have already attained a specified level of training or education;

(f) people with certain physical handicaps or disadvantages of height or weight are not accepted in some occupations;

(g) bankrupts' freedom to engage in commerce is restricted in several ways.

Discrimination of these kinds are generally accepted because they help to prevent harm (as in the case of (a), (b), (d) or (g)), or waste of resources (for instance (e)). For similar reasons, no doubt, the Hawaii Employment Relations Act seems to allow discrimination against someone with a criminal record if the record has a 'substantial relationship to the functions and responsibilities of the ... employment'.

Could a 'rightless' anti-discrimination approach stand up to criticism? The difficulties of drafting legislation of a kind that would bite must be recognised: but they should not be allowed to discredit the principle. Declarations of principle may not be totally without effect in changing attitudes, as the human rights movement has shown. If sensible anti-discrimination principles could be substituted for naïve ideas about rights, this in itself would be an advance. The general principle might be that decisions or selections which might be contrary to the interests or wishes of an individual should not be influenced by information about offences committed by that person unless:

(a) the information rests either on a court's finding of guilt or on an admission by that person (the latter being necessary to cover admissions under diversionary procedures and admissions in applications to decision-makers);

and

(b) the information gives reasonable grounds for fearing that a favourable decision would increase the risk of

(i) serious harm to, or loss by, other people;

or (ii) serious harm to, or loss by, the person himself (for example if a person with a conviction for misuse of heroin applied for a job involving charge of dangerous drugs);

or (iii) damage to the reputation of an agency;

or (iv) detriment to the effective functioning of an agency of law-enforcement.

Proviso (b)(ii) is open to obvious criticism. Why should the principle be so paternalistic as to interfere with the wishes of someone who is willing to take the risk involved in exposing himself to further temptation? One answer could be that if he succumbed the result would not be what Bentham called a 'self-regarding offence', but would entail trouble for others, demands on resources, whether law-enforcement manpower or treatment facilities, and damage to the reputation of the agency concerned. A bolder answer would be simply to defend paternalism where serious harm to the individual is likely: after all, 'paternalism' is yet another rhetorically loaded word. But sacrificing proviso (b)(ii) would not be disastrous for the general principle.

As for damage to an agency's reputation ((b)(iii)), this could be criticised as a ground for discrimination by arguing that it means sacrificing the interests or wishes of an individual to the prejudices of an ill-informed public. In a recent British incident a public relations officer who was a defender of paedophilia and an admitted paedophile was dismissed by an agency for this reason although its work was concerned entirely with adults. The agency seemed to think that his self-publicised views on paedophilia would be detrimental to its image; and in the present state of public opinion this belief must be regarded as very reasonable. Suppose that he had been merely a self-confessed homosexual and defender of homosexuality, and that public opinion were as condemnatory of homosexuality as it was until recently in Britain, and still is in some countries. People who are tolerant of homosexuality might well argue that the employee should not suffer because of this unenlightened attitude. The agency could reply that however unenlightened its public might be, it had to operate in this context for the present. It might well ask why it should sacrifice its interests — which were in this case philanthropic — to benefit an employee whose chances of other kinds of employment were reasonably good, especially when by employing, or continuing to employ, him it would lessen the help which it could give to other people. This argument would of course be much weaker if the employer were in business entirely or mainly with a view to his own interests, or if the result of his policy were to make it very difficult for the individual to find any job. But as an answer it cannot be completely discredited.

'Detriment to the effective functioning of an agency of law-enforcement' ((b)(iv)) is intended to cover, for example, decisions by prosecutors, courts and defence counsel before and during trial and at the sentencing stage; the policy of a probation officer or parole officer in handling probationers or parolees; and the degree of freedom allowed by custodial institutions to individual inmates. The last of these examples is the most controversial, and the most in need of explication by carefully scrutinised rules.

What the general principle could exclude without exception is discrimination which is justifiable only on retributive or denunciatory grounds. Even a pure punisher cannot advocate supplementing a legal sentence with discrimination which has no practical justification. Certainly the form of retributivism which I have described as tenable in Chapter 2 means that either discrimination is part of the expressly provided penalty or it is not *retributively* justified. If a legislature persists in the practice of declaring certain offenders to have forfeited certain civil rights, then these are part of the retributive punishment; but no undeclared form of discrimination can be. Even in the case of prescribed forfeitures, the legislators need to consider whether they are prescribing them for practical (e.g., deterrent) purposes or retributive reasons. As for denouncers, they too must accept that if discrimination is to play any important part in denouncing crimes, it must be publicly ordered at the time of sentence. Undeclared discrimination is usually known only to the discriminators and the discriminated, and is therefore of negligible denunciatory value.

With all its difficulties, this seems a sounder approach than disputation about the existence, forfeiture or curtailment of offenders' rights. The question whether one should ever discriminate against someone because of a past offence, and if so in what circumstances, brings the issue down from the level of ethical metaphysics to that of practical morality.

SUMMARY

To sum up: I have argued that while the concept of 'rights' has been a powerful rhetorical device for the improvement of human conditions, including those of prisoners, it needs a critical examination, even at the risk of being labelled reactionary. There can be no dispute about the reality of man-made rights which are embodied in statutes, contracts or other documents with legal force; but the same cannot be said about 'natural rights', whose status is extremely debatable. As for rights embodied in international conventions or declarations, they are not so much rights as persuasive instruments for the creation of statutory rights, which is their intention. Even if one accepts the idea of a natural right, it is not necessarily immune from surrender or waiver by consent, from forfeiture or curtailment. When one right conflicts with another, one or both have to give ground.

The notion of natural rights is thus not as solid a foundation as it appears. More solid would be a moral principle that there should be no discrimination against categories of people, including offenders, without practical justification, 'practical' being used as a term which excludes 'retributive' or 'denunciatory'. Such a principle would admittedly be less sweeping and inspiring than the assertion of inalienable natural rights. It would leave room for argument about the practical need for certain forms of discrimination by law-enforcement agencies, including prisons, and by employers. But at least the argument could be based on practicalities rather than faith.

9 Simplifying

The last chapter is one more illustration of the chronic problem of penology. Improvements seem to be achievable only if enough people can be persuaded to adopt moral positions which are both simple and extreme: the assertion of inalienable rights, the disowning of deterrence, the abandonment of treatment, the denial of dangerousness. What is disquieting is not merely the reduction of penology to a political level, in which rhetoric takes the place of reasoning. It is the very real possibility that the whole subject will be discredited both amongst practitioners − by which I mean sentencers, administrators and those whose job it is to handle offenders − and also in the eyes of research workers and moral philosophers who, if not disillusioned, would make genuine contributions.

In *Behaviour and Misbehaviour* I ridiculed criminologists whose ambition is to produce 'general theories' which would explain not merely all crime but also all 'deviance'. I am equally sceptical about the possibility of arriving at a simple, coherent position which will tell us how we should solve all the moral problems presented by law enforcement.

If simplicity and coherence were all-important, we could be content with a rigidly retributive penal system, in which every offence would have its fixed price, with no mitigating discounts or aggravating surcharges. Sentencers would have few worries about the effects of their sentences on offenders and the public; and these worries would be confined to the amount of suffering to be aimed at for different offences, or the problem presented by offenders who could suffer no more. No attempt would be made to incapacitate dangerous offenders from repeating their offences. Stigma, being an unprescribed side-effect, would be treated as natural punishment, and not allowed to mitigate intentional penalties.

This is not to ridicule the retributive approach in all its forms. As a distributive principle it should protect the innocent from penalties and stigma, if not from commitment to mental hospitals or disqualification for certain activities. As a limiting principle it sets bounds to penalties which are intended to correct or deter. It forces us to be sparing with measures intended to protect the public; and to take predictable stigma into account when sentencing the guilty. The rule-theory of retribution should make us ask whether this or that form of discrimination against offenders is part of the prescribed penalty or a practical necessity; and if the answer is 'neither' it should make us doubt the justification for it. And it is a retributive approach to justice which values consistency in sentencing.

To carry the retributive approach further, however, and rely on desert as the positive justification for what we do to offenders, has little more than simplicity to recommend it; and the price of its simplicity is its sterility. The instrumental approach at least has a constructive aim, the reduction of crime. It may be over-optimistic: corrective measures may seldom be effective; general deterrents may be less effective than we would like; protective sentences may be effective only at a heavy price. But similar objections do not discourage us from trying to reduce disease, poverty and other social evils.

It is the denunciatory approach which is the most falsely seductive. It offers an escape from the sterility of retribution, yet has to assume a retributive audience. It promises subtler reductive benefits than correction and deterrence, in the form of moral education, but with an even worse cost-benefit ratio. Its less ambitious version presents sentencing as a satisfying ceremonial for a small audience: a semi-private funeral.

This does not rule out eclecticism. There are occasions on which a sentence has a valuable expressive function, just as there are occasions on which it is obviously needed to protect or deter. The eclectic can even argue that now and again he has to deal with a degree of wickedness which calls for retributive punishment, provided that he can define that degree. Most of the time, however, he can be no more than a fairly pessimistic reducer, trying at the same time to avoid inconsistency, discrimination, useless stigma, misdiagnoses of dangerousness and the penalising of the excusable.

References

ADAMS, S. (1961) 'The PICO Project' in *The Sociology of Punishment and Correction*, ed. N. Johnston *et al.*, Wiley, New York, 1962.

ADLEY, R. *et al.* (1979) *Take It or Leave It: report of a study group on shoplifting*, Stones Printers, Milford-on-Haven.

AMERICAN FRIENDS' SERVICE COMMITTEE (1971) *Struggle for Justice*, Hill and Wang, New York.

ARGYLE M. (1964) see WALKER, N. D. and ARGYLE, M. (1964).

BAXTER, R. and NUTTALL, C. (1975) 'Severe sentences no deterrent to crime?' in *New Society, 31*, 639, 11ff.

BECCARIA, C. B. (1764) *Dei Delitti e delle Pene*, tr. as *Of Crimes and Punishments*, J. Almon, London, 1767.

BENTHAM, J. (1789) *An Introduction to the Principles of Morals and Legislation*, T. Payne, London.

BERKOWITZ, L. and WALKER, N. D. (1967) 'Laws and moral judgments' in *Sociometry, 30*, 410ff, reproduced in *Law and the Behavioral Sciences*, edd. L. M. Friedman and S. Macaulay, The Bobbs-Merrill Company, Inc., 1969.

BEYLEVELD, D. (1978) *The Effectiveness of General Deterrents against Crime: an annotated bibliography of evaluative research*, Institute of Criminology, Cambridge (microfiche).

BOSANQUET, B. (1918) *Some Suggestions in Ethics*, Macmillan, London.

BOSHIER, R. and JOHNSON, D. (1974) 'Does conviction affect employment opportunities?' in *British Journal of Criminology, 14*, 3, 264ff.

BOTTOMS, A. E. (1977) 'Reflections on the renaissance of dangerousness': Inaugural Lecture in *Howard Journal, XVI,* 16, 70ff.

BUIKHUISEN, W. and DIJKSTERHUIS, F. P. H. (1971) 'Delinquency and stigmatization' in *British Journal of Criminology, 11,* 2, 185ff.

BUIKHUISEN, W. (1974) 'General deterrence: research and theory' in *Abstracts on Criminology and Penology, 14,* 285ff.

BUTLER, Lord (Chairman) (1975) *Report of the Committee on Mentally Abnormal Offenders,* Cmnd. 6244, H.M.S.O., London.

CANADIAN LAW REFORM COMMISSION (1976) 'Our criminal law: report of the Commission on Principles of Criminal Law' in *Canadian Journal of Criminology and Corrections, 18.*

CHILDREN AND YOUNG PERSONS ACT 1933 (England & Wales) H.M.S.O., London.

CHILDREN AND YOUNG PERSONS ACT 1963 (England & Wales) H.M.S.O., London.

COKE, E. (1642) *The Second Part of the Institutes of the Laws of England,* Flesher and Young, London.

COMMITTEE FOR THE STUDY OF INCARCERATION (1976) *Doing Justice,* ed. A. von Hirsch, Hill and Wang, New York.

COOPER, D. (1974) *The Grammar of Living: an explanation of political acts,* Allen Lane, London.

CORNISH, D. B. and CLARKE, R. V. G. (1975) *Residential Treatment and its Effects on Delinquency,* Home Office Research Study No. 32, H.M.S.O. London.

COUNCIL OF EUROPE (1963) *The European Convention on Human Rights* (collected texts) Strasbourg.

CRANSTON, M. (1973) *What are Human Rights?,* The Bodley Head, London.

CRIMINAL JUSTICE AMENDMENT ACT 1975 (New Zealand).

CRIMINAL RECORDS ACT 1970 (Canada).

CROSS, R. (1963) 'Faults in the English law' in *The Listener*, 12 September.

CROSS, R. (1971) *The English Sentencing System* (1st ed.) Butterworths, London; 2nd ed., Butterworths, London, 1975.

DAMASKA, M. R. (1968) 'Adverse legal consequences of convictions and their removal: a comparative study' in *Journal of Criminal Law, Criminology and Police Science, 59,* 3, 374ff and 542ff.

DENNING, Lord (1954) see ROYAL COMMISSION ON CAPITAL PUNISHMENT (1954).

DEPARTMENT OF HEALTH AND SOCIAL SECURITY (1976) *A Review of the Mental Health Act 1959,* Cmnd. 7320, H.M.S.O., London.

DEVLIN, P. (1959) *The Enforcement of Morals,* Maccabean Lecture in Jurisprudence, reproduced as a chapter in *The Enforcement of Morals,* Oxford University Press, London, 1959.

DREHER, E. (1964) *Report,* Proceedings of the 9th International Congress on Penal Law, The Hague.

DURKHEIM, E. (1893) *De la division du travail social,* Paris, tr. as *The Division of Labour in Society,* G. Simpson, Free Press, Glencoe, 1930.

EMPLOYMENT RELATIONS ACT 1976 (Hawaii).

EUROPEAN COMMISSION OF HUMAN RIGHTS (1973) Report on Application No. 4451/70, *Golder v. United Kingdom,* Strasbourg.

EXCERPTA CRIMINOLOGICA (1965), Excerpta Criminologica Foundation, Leiden, *5,* 4, 644ff.

FEINBERG, J. (1970) *Doing and Deserving,* Princeton University Press.

FITZGERALD, P. J. (1962) *Criminal Law and Punishment,* Clarendon Press, Oxford.

GARDINER, Lord (Chairman) (1972) *Living It Down: the problem of old convictions,* report of a Committee set up by JUSTICE, The Howard League for Penal Reform and the National Association for the Care and Resettlement of Offenders, Stevens, London.

GEIS, G. (1978) 'Legal restrictions on media coverage of deviance in England and America: the case of rape' in *Mass Media and Deviance,* ed. C. Winick, Sage, Beverly Hills.

GIBBS, J. P. (1975) *Crime, Punishment and Deterrence,* Elsevier, New York.

GROSS, H. (1979) *A Theory of Criminal Justice,* Oxford University Press, London.

HART, H. L. A. (1955) 'Are there any natural rights?' in *Philosophical Review, LXIV,* 175ff.

HART, H. L. A. (1965) *The Morality of the Criminal Law:* two lectures, Oxford University Press, London.

HART, H. L. A. (1968) *Punishment and Responsibility:* essays in the philosophy of law, Oxford University Press, London.

HEILBRON, Mrs. R. (Chairman) (1975) *Report of Advisory Group on the Law of Rape,* Cmnd. 6352, H.M.S.O., London.

HIRSCH, A. von (1976) see COMMITTEE FOR THE STUDY OF INCARCERATION (1976).

HOBBES, T. (1651) *Leviathan,* Andrew Crooke, London.

HOHFELD, W. N. (1913) 'Some fundamental legal conceptions as applied in judicial reasoning' in *Yale Law Journal, XXIII.*

HOME OFFICE (1961) *Compensation for Victims of Violence,* Report of a Working Party, Cmnd. 1406, H.M.S.O., London.

HOME OFFICE (1964) *The Prison Rules, England and Wales,* Statutory Instrument 1964, No. 388 (as amended).

HONDERICH, T. (1969) *Punishment: the supposed justifications* (1st ed.) Hutchinson, London; 2nd ed., Penguin, Harmondsworth, 1976.

HUMAN RIGHTS ACT 1975–76 (Canada)

HUNTER, Lord (Chairman) (1975) *Crime and the Prevention of Crime,* Report of the Scottish Council on Crime, H.M.S.O., Edinburgh.

KANT, I. (1797) *Rechtslehre* Voss, Leipzig; tr. as *The Philosophy of Law* by W. Hastie, Clarke, Edinburgh, 1887.

KASSEBAUM, G. *et al.* (1971) *Prison Treatment and Parole Survival,* Wiley, London.

KITTRIE, N. (1971) *The Right to be Different,* The Johns Hopkins Press, Baltimore.

KOZOL, H. *et al.* (1972) 'The diagnosis and treatment of dangerousness' in *Crime and Delinquency, 18,* 371ff.

KVARACEUS, W. C. (1966) *Anxious Youth,* Columbus, Ohio.

LEWIS, C. S. (1953) 'The humanitarian theory of punishment' in *University of Melbourne Law Review,* 228ff.

LOCKE, J. (1690) *Two Treatises of Government,* Churchill, London.

MANNHEIM, H. (1939) *The Dilemma of Penal Reform,* Routledge, London.

MARGRAVE-JONES, R. D. (1959) 'Taking other offences into consideration' in *Criminal Law Review,* 18ff and 108ff.

MARTIN, J. and WEBSTER, D. (1971) *The Social Consequences of Conviction,* Heinemann, London.

MARTINSON, R. M. (1974) 'What works?' in *The Public Interest, 35,* 22ff.

MAYHEW, P. *et al.* (1976) *Crime as Opportunity,* Home Office Research Study No. 34, H.M.S.O., London.

MEGARGEE, E. I. (1976) 'The prediction of dangerous behaviour' in *Criminal Justice and Behavior, 3,* 1, 3ff.

MENTAL HEALTH ACT 1959 (England and Wales).

MILL, J. S. (1859) *On Liberty,* Parker, London.

MOBERLY, E. S. (1978) *Suffering, Innocent and Guilty,* Society for the Promotion of Christian Knowledge, London.

MOBERLY, W. (1968) *The Ethics of Punishment,* Faber and Faber, London.

MONTESQUIEU, C. de S. (1748) *L'esprit des lois,* tr. as *The Spirit of the Laws,* Nourse and Vaillant, London, 1750.

NADIN-DAVIS, P. (1979) *Erasing the Mark of Cain*, thesis submitted for the LL.M., University of Dalhousie, Nova Scotia (unpublished).

NOZICK, R. (1974) *Anarchy, State and Utopia*.

PONTELL, H. N. (1978) 'Deterrence: theory versus practice' in *Criminology, 16*, 1, 3ff.

POPPER, K. (1959) *The Logic of Scientific Discovery*, Hutchinson, London.

RACHMAN, S. (1971) *The Effects of Psychotherapy*, Pergamon Press, Oxford.

RAPHAEL, D. D. (1976) *Problems of Political Philosophy*, Macmillan, London.

REHABILITATION OF OFFENDERS ACT 1974 (United Kingdom), H.M.S.O., London.

REPETTO, T. A. (1974) *Residential Crime*, Ballinger, Cambridge, Massachusetts.

ROSS, H. L. (1970) 'Determining the social effects of a legal reform: the British breathalyser crackdown of 1967' in *American Behavioral Scientist, 13*, 4, 493ff.

ROYAL COMMISSION ON CAPITAL PUNISHMENT (1954), *Minutes of Evidence*, H.M.S.O., London.

ROYAL COMMISSION ON THE PENAL SYSTEM IN ENGLAND AND WALES (1967), *Minutes of Evidence*, H.M.S.O., London.

SARBIN, T. (1967) The dangerous individual: an outcome of social identity transformations' in *British Journal of Criminology, 7*, 3, 285ff.

SCHUR, E. M. (1963) *Narcotic Addiction in Britain and America*, Tavistock Publications, London.

SCHWARTZ, R. D. and ORLEANS, S. (1967) 'On legal sanctions' in *University of Chicago Law Review, XXXIV*, 274ff.

SCHWARTZ, R. D. and SKOLNICK, J. H. (1962) 'Two studies of legal stigma' in *Social Problems, 10*, 132ff.

SCOTTISH COUNCIL ON CRIME (1975) see HUNTER, Lord (1975).

SPREUTELS, J. P. (1977) *Reasons given for Criminal*

Sentences, thesis submitted for the Diploma in Legal Studies, University of Cambridge (unpublished).

STACE, M. (1976) 'Name suppression and the Criminal Justice Amendment Act 1975' in *British Journal of Criminology, 16,* 4, 395ff.

STALLYBRASS, W. T. (1945) 'A comparison of the general principles of criminal law in England with the 'Progetto Definitivo di un nuovo codice penale' of Alfredo Rocco' in *The Modern Approach to Criminal Law,* edd. L. Radzinowicz and J. W. C. Turner, Macmillan, London.

STEER, D. (1967) see WALKER, N. D., HAMMOND, W. and STEER, D. (1967).

STEIN, P. and SHAND, J. (1974) *Legal Values in Western Society,* Edinburgh University Press, Edinburgh.

STEPHEN, J. F. (1873) *Liberty, Equality, Fraternity,* Smith, Elder, London.

STEPHEN, J. F. (1883) *A History of the Criminal Law of England,* 3 vols., Macmillan, London.

TAY, A. E. -S. (1978) 'Marxism, socialism and human rights' in *Human Rights,* edd. E. Kamenka and A. E. -S. Tay, Arnold, London.

THOMAS, D. A. (1970) *Principles of Sentencing* (1st ed.) Heinemann, London; 2nd ed., Heinemann, London, 1979.

TWENTIETH CENTURY FUND TASK FORCE ON CRIMINAL SENTENCING (1976) *Fair and Certain Punishment,* Twentieth Century Fund, Inc., McGraw-Hill, New York.

UNITED NATIONS (1948) Universal Declaration of Human Rights, *United Nations Bulletin,* 1 January 1949, 6ff.

WALDO, G. P. and CHIRICOS, T. E. (1972) 'Perceived penal sanction and self-reported criminality ...' in *Social Problems, 19,* 4, 522ff.

WALKER, N. D. and ARGYLE, M. (1964) 'Does the law affect moral judgments?' in *British Journal of Criminology, 4,* 6, 570ff., reproduced in *Perception in Criminology,* edd. R. L. Henshel and R. A. Silverman, Columbia University Press, 1975.

WALKER, N. D., HAMMOND, W. and STEER, D. (1967)

'Repeated violence' in *Criminal Law Review,* 465ff.

WALKER, N. D. (1967) see BERKOWITZ, L..and WALKER, N. D. (1967).

WALKER, N. D. (1968) *Crime and Punishment in Britain* (2nd ed.) Edinburgh University Press, Edinburgh.

WALKER, N. D. (1968) *Crime and Insanity in England* (vol. 1) Edinburgh University Press, Edinburgh.

WALKER, N. D. (1969) *Sentencing in a Rational Society,* Allen Lane, The Penguin Press, London.

WALKER, N. D. (1977) *Behaviour and Misbehaviour,* Blackwell, Oxford; Basic Books, New York.

WILLCOCK, H. D. and STOKES, J. (1963) *Deterrents and Incentives to Crime among Youths aged 15–21 years,* Part II, Tables, Government Social Survey, London.

WILLETT, T. C. E. (1964) *Criminal on the Road: a study of serious motoring offences and those who commit them,* Tavistock, London.

WILLETT, T. C. E. (1975) *Drivers after Sentence,* Heinemann, London.

WOLFENDEN, Sir J. F. (Chairman) (1975) *Report of Committee on Homosexual Offences and Prostitution,* Cmnd. 247, H.M.S.O., London.

WOOTTON, Baroness (Chairman) (1970) *Non-Custodial and Semi-Custodial Penalties,* Report of Sub-Committee of the Advisory Council on the Penal System, H.M.S.O., London.

ZIMRING, F. E. and HAWKINS, G. J. (1973) *Deterrence: the legal threat in crime control,* University of Chicago Press.

Index